WHEN
THE WORLD
RUNS DRY

Also by Nancy F. Castaldo

River Wild: An Activity Guide to North American Rivers
Oceans: An Activity Guide for Ages 6–9
The Story of Seeds
Back from the Brink: Saving Animals from Extinction

WHEN THE WORLD RUNS DRY

EARTH'S WATER IN CRISIS

Nancy F. Castaldo

Algonquin Young Readers
2022

Published by
Algonquin Young Readers
an imprint of Algonquin Books of Chapel Hill
Post Office Box 2225
Chapel Hill, North Carolina 27515-2225

a division of
Workman Publishing
225 Varick Street
New York, New York 10014

PHOTO CREDITS: Becker1999/flickr: p. 64; Lucie A. Castaldo: p. 129; Nancy F. Castaldo: pp. vii, xv, 11, 17, 53, 56, 63, 74, 79, 83, 92, 104, 112, 121, 146, 149, 161; Chantel Comardelle (used by permission): p. 118; Dave Cooper: p. 38; NYSDEC: p. 27; Shutterstock/INTOtheSIBERIA: endsheets; Shutterstock/R_Tee: p. xii.

AUDIENCE: ages 10 and up; grades 5 and up

LIBRARY OF CONGRESS CATALOGING-IN-PUBLICATION DATA
Names: Castaldo, Nancy F. (Nancy Fusco), 1962– author.
Title: When the world runs dry : earth's water in crisis / Nancy F. Castaldo.
Description: First edition. | Chapel Hill, North Carolina : Algonquin Young Readers, 2022. | Includes bibliographical references and index.
Summary: "A narrative nonfiction account of the worldwide water crisis, explaining what's happening to the world's water supply, from industrial pollution to harmful algal blooms, and what kids can do about it"—Provided by publisher.
Identifiers: LCCN 2021040517 | ISBN 9781616209711 (hardcover) | ISBN 9781643752273 (ebook)
Subjects: LCSH: Water-supply—Juvenile literature. | Water—Pollution—Juvenile literature. | Water quality—Juvenile literature.
Classification: LCC TD348 .C325 2022 | DDC 363.739/4—dc23
LC record available at https://lccn.loc.gov/2021040517

10 9 8 7 6 5 4 3 2 1
First Edition

In memory of Jassmine McBride

And in memory of my mom, Annette, the
first water protector in my life

Only when . . . the last stream has been

poisoned will you realize you cannot eat money.

—Cree proverb

The twentieth century was about oil

but the twenty-first century will be about water.
—consumer advocate Erin Brockovich

Spring water is justice, colourless and clear.
—Swedish poet Karin Boye,

translated by Jenny Nunn

TABLE OF CONTENTS

WHEN
THE WORLD
RUNS DRY

INTRODUCTION: YOU JUST TURN ON THE FAUCET, RIGHT?

WHEN YOU GET UP IN THE MORNING and turn on the faucet of your bathroom sink, you can probably trust that water is going to flow out through the tap. The same goes for the showerhead, the kitchen sink, the toilet, the garden hose, the dishwasher. You may not know where the water comes from, exactly, or how it's been treated, but you expect clean, safe water to flow, like magic, whenever you need it.

But imagine waking up one day and finding there isn't any water flowing through the tap—or the water coming out of the faucet is toxic. No water to brush your teeth, shower, or flush your toilet. More importantly, no water to *drink*. And it's not just your house that's affected. There's no water flowing out of your neighbors' faucets, either. In fact, your whole town has lost its access to water. What would *you* do?

You'd probably manage pretty well during the first hour—or even the first day or two—with the liquids you stockpiled in your home. But as the days go on, the difficulty increases. Store shelves empty in town after town as everyone competes for bottled water. If the scarcity continues, you may have to survive on government deliveries of rationed water that might not be enough to meet all your needs.

How many days could go by before you would panic? What if there was no water to drink or use for bathing for weeks, months, or even years?

This isn't a far-fetched scenario. In fact, it's happening in places all around the world—from Flint, Michigan, to Cape Town, South Africa.

And this loss of water isn't just inconvenient. It's life-threatening. There are many things we could live without, but water isn't one of them.

WATER IS LIFE

Wenona T. Singel is a citizen of and the chief appellate justice for the Little Traverse Bay Bands of Odawa Indians. In the fall of 2018, she lent her voice in Flint, Michigan—the site of a severe ongoing water crisis—to the discussion about the need and right of all living creatures to have access to clean water. "In the Anishinaabe culture, water is sacred—water is life," Singel said. "Water has its own spirit."

Members of her tribe and other Indigenous cultures believe that water is a living being with a spirit that deserves respect. Modeling the beaded Thunder Woman on the medallion she wore around her neck, Singel spoke with clarity and conviction about our relationship with water, saying that it is with each of us inside the womb of our mother and is released when each of us is born.

This view of water as a life-giving force is reflected in the "Waters" section of Ohenten Kariwatekwen, often called the Haudenosaunee Thanksgiving Address. The title means "words spoken before all others," and the address is recited at the opening of important gatherings. This translation is of the Mohawk version that was published in 1993 by the Six Nations Iroquois Cultural Center in Onchiota, New York: "We give thanks to all the waters of the world for quenching our thirst and providing us with strength. Water is life. We know its power in many forms—waterfalls and rain, mists and streams, rivers and

Wenona Singel shares how the water crisis affects everyone, especially Tribal nations.

oceans. With one mind, we send greetings and thanks to the spirit of Water. Now our minds are one."

As the address says, *water is life*. We all need it to live, and not just for showering, brushing teeth, or flushing the toilet. About 60 percent of the human body is made up of water, and every human cell needs water to function. Water is crucial for circulation and digestion, and for transporting nutrients to every part of the body. In normal circumstances, a person can live roughly one week without water. In extreme conditions, like desert heat, that timeline is shorter.

And humans aren't alone in terms of relying on this precious resource. Water is essential to all life on planet Earth, from the largest elephant that drinks about 50 gallons (189 liters) each day to the small desert spadefoot toad, which wraps itself in a mucous membrane to conserve water while estivating underground until it emerges ten months later after a rainstorm.

We also need water to create the energy that powers our lives and all the products we use and eat. Every power plant uses water. Every farm uses water. Every industry uses water. It takes 1,400 gallons (5,300 liters) of water to produce a single meal of a burger, fries, and a soft drink. How? Water is used to grow the food and supply the drink for the cows. Water is used to grow the potatoes for the fries and power the machinery at the plant that turns those potatoes into fries. Water is used directly not only in the soft drink but also in the industrial process of producing the can or bottle that contains it. And it's not just food that sucks up water—it takes over 2,000 gallons (7,570 liters) to produce one pair of jeans, and it requires three times more water to make a plastic bottle than the water it contains.

Then there's all the water we use in our daily lives. The average person in a developed country uses about 60 to 80 gallons (227–302 liters) of water each day for washing, drinking, cooking, and flushing the toilet. It takes about 25 gallons (95 liters) of water for a ten-minute shower, and a single toilet flush can use up to 7 gallons (26 liters).

These water requirements might all be fine if there were a never-ending supply of water. But there isn't, and people all over the world are feeling the strain and finding themselves without enough fresh water for them to live comfortably.

THE WATER CRISIS

The world is home to nearly eight billion people. According to UNICEF, approximately six thousand children die each day from unsafe drinking water and poor sanitation. In addition, UNICEF reports that worldwide, children under five years of age are roughly twenty times as likely to perish from water-related illnesses as from armed conflicts.

In the United States alone, more than two million people live without running water and indoor plumbing, including many families on the Navajo Nation reservation in the Southwest. There are people in California and New Hampshire who have turned on their faucet to find their taps dry, while families along the Texas-Mexico border worry they won't have enough water to fight fires.

Stories about the lack of water are coming from around the globe, not just the United States. In South Africa, residents of Cape Town have wrestled for years with preventing Day Zero, the day the city could run out of water. In India, the country's sixth-largest city, Chennai, resorted to a token system to ration water in 2019 when taps there ran dry. And in Kenya, women and young girls walk miles to reach wells in the sub-Saharan Africa heat to get water for their families each morning. When they reach the well or watering hole, they jockey for position, often competing with cattle and honeybees for each sip. They fill buckets, cans, or bottles, then walk the same hot miles home, careful not to spill a single, vital drop. Globally, clean water is out of reach for almost two billion people, causing many women and children to have to walk on average 3.5 miles (5.6 kilometers) to get water each day.

Other people, like families in Flint, Michigan, have suffered from a different type of water stress—toxic water. Their drinking water was poisoned in 2014 by lead and harmful bacteria when the city changed the water supply from water sourced from Lake Huron and the Detroit River to the Flint River. Residents in a town in Pennsylvania found their water was poisoned with chemicals used in the process of extracting natural gas. A half million people in Ohio discovered their water had been contaminated by agricultural run-off. And residents in upstate New York learned that the water they had been drinking for years contained chemicals used to make plastic at a nearby factory.

Stories involving water scarcity or toxicity are all around us. Hardly a day passes when there isn't a story, or *multiple* stories, about water in the news. Some of these stories are obvious—those about drought, pollution, or contamination. They are the stories with the word *water* right in the headline.

But water is an integral part of many news stories that don't at first glance seem to be about water. There are stories of refugees in South America fleeing areas that can no longer support farming because of drought, or wars that started partly because of conflict over the scarcity of water.

Many stories filling our news feeds make it clear: Water is in crisis. But why? Before we can understand the current water crisis, we must look at our water infrastructure—how for millennia humans have harnessed this precious resource for everything from irrigating crops to milling grain to quenching our thirst.

OUR WATER INFRASTRUCTURE

Water is everywhere. As the Haudenosaunee Thanksgiving Address signals, it fills our oceans, our rivers, and our streams. It flows deep under the earth. It moves through a cycle of use and reuse, with value all along the way. It is our drinking water, wastewater, stormwater, and gray water. It falls as rain, sleet, and snow. And for thousands of years, we've innovated ways to bring water to villages and cities.

Aqueducts were built by early civilizations in Egypt and India to transport water to populated areas, enabling people to live some distance from a direct water source. Instead of living and planting crops near a well or collecting rainwater, people could settle in more urban areas and have water delivered to them via human-made pipes and channels.

Roman aqueducts constructed between 312 BC and AD 226 were engineering marvels. They carried fresh water through pipes, tunnels, canals, and bridges to ancient cities for drinking, bathing, and irrigation. They supplied Roman villas, gardens, farms, city baths, and fountains, and they were a source of water for up to a million Roman people.

Much of the modern water system in the United States has been built on the principles that those ancient civilizations used: A series of pipes and canals bring water from lakes, rivers, or beneath the earth to towns and cities. America's rapid transformation during the 1800s from an agrarian nation to an industrialized one spurred the development of this infrastructure. Urban areas like New York City moved away from obtaining water from shallow wells or small reservoirs within the city to importing water from outside it to meet the demands of a growing population. And the water had to be clean. In 1908, physician and water treatment expert John Laing Leal, from nearby New Jersey, developed the use of chlorine to disinfect the country's water supply, and today we have more treatment methods.

Our modern water infrastructure—a sophisticated system that utilizes pipes, storage facilities, and treatment plants—is the result of

The Urban Water Cycle

The classic model of a freshwater cycle shows how surface water in lakes and rivers evaporates to become rain, which falls on the earth. The rainwater makes its way back into lakes and rivers and then the cycle begins all over again.

Similarly, the urban water cycle describes the process by which water moves through developed areas. Surface water or groundwater is pumped up through wells and passes through water treatment steps in an effort to remove any harmful impurities, like microorganisms. After treatment, the water is distributed through pipes into the city. It is often stored in water towers, sometimes on the roofs of buildings. Citizens use the water for drinking, washing, and other needs. The water leaves our homes through drains and toilets, and the wastewater is cleaned at a treatment facility. Once cleaned, the water reenters the environment.

thousands of years of technological innovations. But this infrastructure is also deeply flawed.

CAUSES OF CRISIS

Our water infrastructure faces numerous challenges. Over time, pipe systems, or waterlines, can become compromised by leaks and corrosion. Water treatment must combat industrial and agricultural pollution. Growing populations demand more water from finite sources. Each of these stresses creates a web of problems.

For example, aging pipes with leaks and other damage can lead to water contamination. When waterlines break, chemicals from industry and other sources can leach into the system. Poor pipe maintenance and water treatment can cause lead and bacteria to enter the water, contributing to rampant health concerns for communities, especially smaller and disadvantaged locales that don't have the funds to replace their pipes.

More than a century of water management in the United States has also disrupted the natural flow and storage of water. The use of dams, pipes, and drilling has drawn water away from communities that need it. For example, in the early 1900s, the federal government subsidized drinking water and irrigation for settlers in the West. This program, however, often created hardships for Indigenous people like those of the Navajo Nation.

Many communities have insufficient water infrastructure (the pipes and related equipment necessary to get water from its source into homes and other buildings). In the 1950s, for example, waterlines were not laid down in African American neighborhoods in Zanesville, Ohio, as they were in white areas. Rural Latinx farming communities, like Seville and East Porterville in California's Central Valley, were discouraged from incorporating because they had "little or no authentic future." This disqualified them from receiving funding for water infra-structure programs. In addition, Indigenous households have a long history of infrastructure challenges. The 2019 *Closing the Water Access Gap in the United States* national report signaled that these house-holds are nineteen times more likely to lack indoor plumbing than white households. Although many of these injustices took place in the past, they've had a long reach and continue to adversely affect many communities.

Another factor pushing us to the point of crisis is population growth. The number of people on planet Earth increased from one billion in 1800 to nearly eight billion in 2020. That increase is strain-ing access to an ever-decreasing resource. Although our planet is 70 percent water, more than 96 percent of that water is salt water, which—unless it goes through the desalination process to remove the salt—cannot be used for drinking or agriculture. That means that eight billion people compete for the remaining 4 percent of Earth's water. This rapid growth in demand also increases the pressure on the aging infrastructure.

Climate change is another contributing factor. Warming tempera-tures cause drought around the planet, freshwater glaciers melt into the oceans, sea level rises, and rivers dry up. Severe weather wreaks havoc far and wide. Violent storms create water runoff that doesn't soak into the soil but instead flows out to the sea or contaminates freshwater supplies. The world's wet regions are getting wetter, and the world's dry areas are getting drier. These changes heighten water stress, causing risks to human health, food supplies, and economies while also compromising the environment.

And much of the fresh water that remains is being polluted. Industrial, agricultural, and pharmaceutical waste is seeping into our water supply. Lead infiltrates the water from untreated or aging pipes.

According to the United Nations (UN), as of 2020, more people world-wide were dying each year from contaminated water than from all forms of violence, including war.

WHAT MIGHT THE FUTURE HOLD?

Comparing the ratio of the water that we use with the supply of available water around the globe makes it possible to predict upcoming water stress for each country in the world.

The Water Resources Institute, based in Washington, DC, warns that if water usage rates continue on their current course, in 2040 the ratio of withdrawal of water to supply will soar over 80 percent in North Africa, the Middle East, Spain, and Chile, regions that are already experiencing droughts or other water stress. In addition, many other countries, including the United States, China, Australia, India, and Italy, will also face serious challenges unless changes in water usage and climate action occur.

This global stress is predicted to leave millions of people without enough water to meet their needs.

TIME FOR A CLOSER LOOK

We are in trouble. Water is required for all life on Earth. Having access to water is defined as a human right. But how can we assure that everyone has access to it, given the many problems we're facing?

It's time to take a closer look at the water crisis and how it has played out in communities around the globe. By gaining a deeper understanding of the problems, we can build toward possible solutions.

CHAPTER 1: GETTING THE LEAD OUT— WATER INFRASTRUCTURE PROBLEMS

THE QUALITY OF THE WATER that flows out of your tap depends on how the water was initially treated as well as the construction of the pipes that it passed through to reach you.

If you have municipal water—water that is supplied to all homes and businesses from a central source, like a reservoir—it follows a pathway through pipes from the source to the treatment facility to your home. The treatment facility has filters and chemicals that clean the water before it reaches you. Once there, it enters your plumbing and eventually arrives at your tap.

Problems along the water's pathway, however, could make your water unsafe. Old pipes can deteriorate and release compounds and minerals that pollute your water. Ideally, pipes should be treated with chemicals and coatings so that they do not leach toxic chemicals like copper, iron, or lead into the water supply.

Many pipes underneath our streets and in many older homes were cast with available materials deemed safe at the time of construction. In the United States, lead was commonly used for both service-line pipes that connected water mains to homes and in the solder that was used to connect pipes. Lead, however, is toxic.

Cities began moving away from using lead service-line pipes in the 1920s, and, by the 1950s, most pipes were made from other materials, such as copper or steel. Lead pipes were, however, approved by national plumbing codes into the 1980s. And there are still plenty of lead pipes remaining underneath the streets of America and in household plumbing fixtures. Replacing all the pipes of a city or town is expensive and not every community can afford such a large project. But if not treated properly or removed, lead pipes endanger the health of everyone who drinks the water flowing through them.

In 1986 and 1996 the United States Congress amended the Safe Drinking Water Act. Both of these amendments further protected citizens from lead in plumbing fittings, fixtures, and pipes. Congress passed the Reduction of Lead in Drinking Water Act (RLDWA) in 2011. This legislation lowered the allowable amount of lead that can be found in items defined as lead-free. The 2011 RLDWA provided further protections as well, but it also permitted exceptions for fixtures that do not supply water for human consumption, such as toilets.

LEAD: THE SILENT KILLER

Lead is one of the most hazardous water pollutants. It's a neurotoxin, which means it damages the human neurological system. High levels of lead contribute to behavioral changes, developmental disabilities, increased cardiovascular risks, and cognitive impairment. High blood pressure and kidney damage in adults can also occur. Even short-term overexposure to lead can cause abdominal pain, memory loss, tingling in the hands, and other symptoms.

Children are at the highest risk for lead poisoning. It is especially harmful to their developing brains and, as exposure builds, can contribute to cognitive problems, including learning difficulties and attention deficit disorder.

Lead is particularly insidious because it is odorless and tasteless in water. Often, water is not tested for lead until health problems develop and lead is found in the patient's blood.

And there isn't a quick cure for lead poisoning. There isn't a pill that can erase the damage that comes from exposure. There are only treatments, such as chelation, that can offset very high lead levels in blood. For the most part, doctors can only raise awareness and work to limit future exposure.

If lead concentrations exceed 15 parts per billion (ppb) in more than 10 percent of taps sampled, the US Environmental Protection Agency (EPA) requires public notification and service lines replaced. But sometimes, the public isn't notified until much too late. That's what happened in one of the most publicized and galvanizing water stories in recent years: the water crisis of Flint, Michigan.

CASE STUDY: FLINT, MICHIGAN—GROUND ZERO OF AMERICA'S WATER INFRASTRUCTURE CRISIS

The effects of lead is [sic] insidious,
But I don't want you to pity us,
Or to get rid of us by poisoning us.
But to use your might to do what's right,
Equal protection of the law is a civil right,
Redistribution of resources will change our plight.
—From "The Menace of Lead" by Bunyan Bryant, Ph.D.,
professor emeritus, University of Michigan, and an
environmental justice scholar and researcher

At first glance, Flint looks like many other small cities in the United States. Its downtown has shops, restaurants, and a historic theater for plays, concerts, and movies. Cars park along the main street and people hurry to and from appointments. The city boasts the second-largest art museum in the state and a robust state university campus community.

But beyond downtown, in the nine wards where people should be living, it's clear that Flint has scars. The first were inflicted when the largest manufacturer and employer, General Motors (GM), and other manufacturing businesses began leaving the city in the 1980s and caused sweeping unemployment—and more recent ones followed with the water crisis.

Once called Vehicle City because half its population worked at the GM plants, many streets in Flint are now filled with skeletons of scorched, empty homes with weed-choked gardens and vacant lots where houses once stood. By 2018, only one or two homes were still occupied on some ward streets. Stores were shuttered. The frustration of residents was signaled by the empty water bottles littering the lawn of city hall near the bronze statue of an assembly line autoworker. The statue symbolized the perseverance of Flint's past generations who had fought for labor rights and helped create the middle class in the United States.

What went wrong in Flint? Like so many cities, Flint had an aging water infrastructure. When the city's water source was switched in April 2014, lead from the improperly treated pipes leached into everyone's water supply. Residents were not notified until after the lead was in their bodies.

THE FLINT RIVER

"So later this spring, we will all be drinking Pure Flint Michigan Natural Mineral Water," Flint mayor Dayne Walling said in his State of the City address in March 2014. "The new water will be properly treated, lightly fluoridated, and will taste slightly different than the water from Lake Huron that came through Detroit. Pure Flint Michigan Natural Mineral Water."

Flint's finances were in dire shape after the loss of manufacturing by GM and others. The tax base was dwindling, and the cost of supplying water to residents was rising. To save money, city officials decided to switch water companies from Detroit Water and Sewage to the Karegnondi Water Authority. Before the new connection to Karegnondi could be built, the city turned to the Flint River as a temporary water source.

In his address to Flint residents, Walling put a great spin on the cost-saving measure. But the truth was, using Flint River water was risky. All river water is exposed to unwanted particles, microorganisms, and organic matter that can enter the water easily. Flint River also had a history of pollution from the abundance of local manufacturing facilities, and it has long been naturally high in corrosive chloride that can eat away at lead water pipes—which was especially bad for Flint. Although lead pipes were banned from use in US plumbing systems in 1986, Flint was one of the many cities with older water infrastructures that incorporated them.

Still, the plan went ahead. An engineering firm was hired to prepare the Flint Water Treatment Plant for Flint River water, and Flint Emergency Manager Darnell Earley stated in a March 2014 letter: "We expect that the Flint Water Treatment Plant will be fully operational and capable of treating Flint River water before the date of termination [with Detroit Water and Sewage]."

When the switch occurred, residents complained about the taste, the color, and the rotten-egg smell. But they didn't know it lacked appropriate treatment of the corrosive river water to ensure drinking-water safety, despite Earley's assurance. To save money, phosphoric acid—a chemical that inhibits iron pipe corrosion and prevents lead from leaching—was not added.

So what happened when Flint River water began flowing through the pipes? The chloride corroded the pipes, and toxic lead leached into the water. The people of Flint drank, and also bathed or cooked with, lead-contaminated water. The corrosive water damaged dishwashers, washing machines, and plumbing throughout the city. More seriously, lead entered the bloodstream of everyone who drank the water.

Remember—if lead concentration exceeds 15 ppb in more than 10 percent of taps sampled, the US EPA requires public notification and service lines replaced. Lead levels in Flint exceeded this by twenty times for some homes tested in 2015, with several testing over 100 ppb and one water sample exceeding 1000 ppb. Lee Anne Walters's Flint home was reported to have a lead content of 104 ppb. The testing of 252 out of 300 samples were shipped to Virginia Tech for analysis. Their conclusion found such high lead quantities that Flint water should have failed to meet the EPA Lead and Copper rule. And yet it would take state officials more than a year to inform the public about the high lead levels.

All the while, Flint residents continued drinking contaminated water and also using it for bathing and cooking.

THE DISCOVERY

While local and state officials kept silent, Dr. Mona Hanna-Attisha, a pediatrician at Hurley Medical Center in Flint, revealed the disaster in early autumn of 2015. She was first alerted to a potential problem by a former EPA employee who told her that water engineer and college professor Marc

Edwards and his Virginia Tech team had studied the water and found high levels of lead in the homes of Flint residents. Until that chance conversation Dr. Hanna-Attisha had had no idea of the potentially dire situation. After all, it wasn't unusual for kids growing up in older homes with lead paint to experience some exposure. Even when her patients had shown signs of lead exposure, she hadn't connected the problem to Flint's drinking water. But she soon discovered that some cases she was seeing in her general practice were different: They were originating in the city's drinking water.

Many Flint babies had their blood tested when they were one and two years old as a regular practice. When Dr. Hanna-Attisha investigated the health records of babies born before, during, and after the water switch to the Flint River to discover any abnormalities in their lead levels, she found a spike that the health department had not reported to the public.

Once she made the connection, Dr. Hanna-Attisha couldn't keep silent. She urged everyone to stop drinking Flint water at a press conference in September 2015.

Testing began throughout the city, revealing a water crisis of epic proportions that had an impact on everyone in Flint, young and old. Governor Rick Snyder released a plan in October to provide free filters and water testing for Flint residents.

PUTTING FIRE TO THE KETTLE

The water in Flint resident Tia Ivory's bathroom faucet measured 376 ppb of lead and 1150 ppb of copper in 2016. Both elements were dangerous to her health. Her kitchen results were significantly lower, at 27 ppb of lead and 170 ppb of copper, but they were still far above the EPA's approved percentages. Ivory's lead levels were so high that US Surgeon General

Vice Admiral Vivek H. Murthy visited her home in February 2016. It turned out that her 48507 Flint zip code had one of the highest lead levels in the city.

How do you stay clean and healthy when you can't use your water to drink, bathe, or cook for days, weeks, months, or years? Tia Ivory and her neighbors—many of whom were already suffering from lead poisoning—had to figure that out.

In February 2016, the city hired contractors to begin replacing the pipes. Water bottles were distributed to residents to be used for all their water needs in the meantime. It was difficult, however, to shower, wash their hands, or cook with bottles of water. To keep her teenage son healthy, Ivory sent him away from Flint to live with his dad.

Two years after Murthy's visit, Ivory's water was still not clean. Although the city was working on replacing the pipes under Flint streets, the plumbing in local homes was also in need of replacement. The damage was far-reaching and expensive. Meanwhile, Ivory was still relying on bottled water. She had rashes on her skin and was driving many miles to shower at a local gym.

Ivory's grandparents, like so many others, had come to Flint in the 1940s to work for General Motors. Their house had passed to Ivory, but now—with high city water bills, taxes, and the added expense of purchasing clean water to get through the crisis—she was struggling to keep it. And she wasn't the only one. In May 2017, more than eight thousand Flint residents were at risk of losing their homes if they did not pay the money owed on their water bills. That's right: Through all this, residents were still receiving bills for the toxic water flowing through their pipes. In addition to buying bottled water, they were expected to pay for the water they were using only to flush their toilets. The water crisis became a housing crisis as residents struggled to maintain their properties and their property values.

Ivory spoke out about the crisis at her community center. She knew that the more people who were aware of what her city was going through, the better. Flint residents needed answers and support.

"If we put enough fires to the kettle, it will burn," she said.

LEGIONNAIRES' DISEASE OUTBREAK

While some Flint residents were speaking out, the city's water crisis was taking a deadly new turn. In addition to the lead in the water, there was also bacteria—including the *Legionella pneumophila* bacterium, which can cause a dangerous type of pneumonia called Legionnaires' disease, or simply Legionnaires'. The bacteria, which grows in water, can enter someone's lungs when it's inhaled from a shower or sprinkler system, or if someone chokes on a gulp of contaminated water.

How did this happen in Flint? When chlorine was added to Flint's water supply during treatment in 2014, a chemical reaction occurred in the damaged pipes. The chlorine caused iron to leach from the pipes in addition to lead. Iron promotes the growth of bacteria, including *Legionella pneumophila*. Bacteria levels spiked. More chlorine was added to combat the problem; although it reduced some of the bacteria, it also led to the growth of others. Stagnant water in the lines caused the growth to proliferate even further.

As a result, Flint residents suffered from the third-largest Legionnaires' outbreak in the history of the United States. At least ninety people were infected in 2014 and 2015, and at least thirteen died.

Of the seventy-eight people who survived the initial infection, twenty died over the next two years—and there may have been others. Not everyone who passed away in Flint during that time was tested for *Legionella*. Plus, since the disease mostly targeted people with increased health risks like cancer, heart disease, or diabetes, *Legionella* deaths may have been attributed to other preexisting conditions. The health department claimed that 84 percent of the *Legionella* cases during the outbreak affected residents who had a compromising health condition. Jassmine McBride was one of those residents.

JASSMINE MCBRIDE

On a sunny October day in 2018, Jassmine McBride sat on the porch of her home in Flint, Michigan. Tubing from her nose connected her to an oxygen tank that helped her breathe. When she spoke, her voice was weak.

In August 2014, the then-twenty-four-year-old had visited the local McLaren Flint hospital for a routine appointment to get an iron supplement to treat diabetes. But, unlike with her other appointments, Jassmine didn't return home after this treatment. Instead, her mom received horrific news: The hospital called to ask for permission to resuscitate her daughter. Shocked, Jassmine's mother answered, "Of course," and she rushed to her daughter's bedside.

The scene at the hospital was a nightmare. Jassmine was in intensive care, alive but in a coma and unresponsive. Legionnaires' disease had attacked her lungs. The young woman who had sung with such a bright, loud voice in her high school choir now had barely enough oxygen to live.

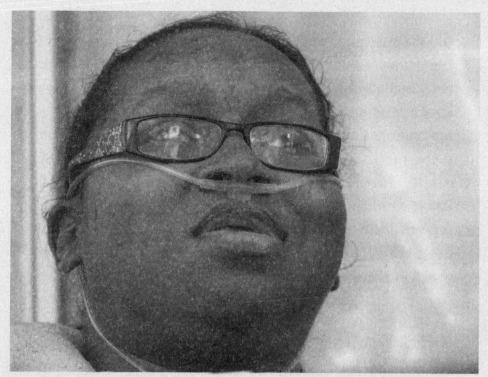

Jassmine McBride suffered fatal complications from Legionnaires' disease caused by the Flint water crisis.

Her mother prayed and waited by her daughter's bedside. Days passed, then weeks. Jassmine remained in intensive care for two months as doctors worked to save her life. When she woke up from the coma in October 2014, she had to relearn everything—from how to eat to how to walk. "She's my miracle," said her mother.

Jassmine returned home that December, but the effects of the disease continued to ravage her body, causing kidney failure, heart failure, and respiratory failure. She passed away just four months after she'd sat on her porch and shared her story on that sunny day in October 2018. In February 2019, she became the thirteenth official victim of Flint's *legionella* crisis as well as the youngest.

SEEKING ANSWERS

Did the switch to the Flint River water cause this outbreak of Legionnaires'? Ask a Flint resident, and they'll likely answer with a quick yes, but the state wanted to investigate. Two studies conducted by Wayne State University's Flint Area Community Health and Environment Partnership found that there was an increased risk of developing Legionnaires' disease throughout Flint. They determined that the change in Flint's drinking water had caused seventy-two of the ninety reported cases of the disease. They also found that there were cases that had gone undetected. Some cases were misdiagnosed as the flu or another respiratory illness in people who were fortunate to recover. These cases didn't require reporting or additional treatment.

The state health department, the same government agency that didn't report the spike of higher lead levels in Flint's children, called the scientists' findings "inaccurate" and "incomplete." The state conducted its own study and blamed McLaren Flint hospital's water distribution system for the outbreak.

THE AFTERMATH

In 2018, years after lead had initially leached from the city's pipes, the scars from Flint's water crisis ran deep in the community. Residents faced ongoing rashes on their legs and arms, vacant homes lined entire streets, many of Flint's schools were shut down, and the signs on water fountains still signaled either clean or unsafe drinking water. Less obvious were the heartache and anxiety left in the wake of the crisis and the impact of developmental issues that compromised the city's children.

Early-childhood education centers and other programs serving kids from two months to five years old sprang up throughout the city to address learning disabilities caused by the high lead levels. Many people moved even though their homes had lost all their value because the houses couldn't be resold without clean, potable water.

But some Flint residents, like sixty-two-year-old retiree Sandra Ballard, found moving during the crisis impossible. "You've got to put first and last month's rent down. Believe me; I wish I could get out of here," she told the *New York Times* in 2016. Sandra died in 2018 without ever leaving Flint.

As for replacing the pipes, the work is ongoing. In October 2018, a marquee in downtown Flint read: MAYOR WEAVER'S FAST START INITIATIVE HAS EXCAVATED 15,031 PIPES AT FLINT HOMES TO DATE!

But much more work needs to be done to replace the estimated twenty thousand pipes running under Flint streets. Once all those are replaced, the pipes in individual homes will have to be changed. And the dishwashers, washing machines, and other appliances destroyed by the toxic water also require replacement.

It has become clear that at the time of the switch, the city's water treatment plant did not have the necessary upgrades in place to treat the Flint River water; in addition, the Michigan Department of Environmental Quality did not require corrosion control. Investigations continued into how the crisis developed and who was responsible. In January 2021, nine officials—including Governor Rick Snyder, Michigan Department of Health and Human Services director Nick Lyon, state-appointed emergency managers Gerald Ambrose and Darnell Earley (also Flint finance manager), Flint Director of Public

Works Howard Croft, and Michigan Department of Health and Human Services official Nancy Peeler—were arrested for their participation in this crisis. Their charges ranged from misdemeanors for neglect of duties to felony charges of involuntary manslaughter. All the accused are presumed innocent, pending the outcome of their trials.

BUILDING A VILLAGE

The Flint crisis was unprecedented, and according to Dr. Hanna-Attisha, it changed our country.

"Because of Flint, there has been an incredible ripple effect," she said in 2018. "People are now testing. They're questioning the safety of their water. They are finding contaminants, whether lead or PFAS [chemicals]. They are no longer believing that our water is safe. That is amazing. That is incredible. People need to be engaged."

Dr. Hanna-Attisha claims that one of the proven lessons of Flint is that it is a "necessity to build a village of folks that are united in whatever cause that you are working toward." She also spoke to the importance of banding together to vote in politicians who advocate for the needs of the community, emphasizing that every voice counts. 💧

IT'S NOT JUST FLINT, MICHIGAN

Flint is not alone in dealing with poisoned water. Towns and cities throughout the United States are facing similar disasters—including in schools. In 2018, the US Government Accountability Office reported that 37 percent of tested school districts had elevated lead levels. Aging pipes, as well as brass fixtures and fittings, may contribute to water with increased lead levels. (Brass is an alloy of copper and zinc, but it can also include aluminum, lead, and arsenic.)

In Arizona, Hopi Elementary School in Phoenix had increased lead levels, and—as in Flint—parents were not informed for over six weeks by the Department of Environmental Quality. Elsewhere in Arizona, Genevieve Boileau-Stockfisch's second-grade classroom at Entz Elementary in Mesa had lead levels that registered at 500 ppb in 2018. A second sample registered at 1300 ppb.

In 2018, Detroit, Michigan, shut down water to its more than one hundred schools, all of which had elevated lead and copper levels. About fifty thousand students used water coolers instead of water fountains until more than five hundred hydration stations with built-in filters were installed a year later.

What to Do If Lead Is Found in Your School's Water

1. Ask a school official if filters will be installed.

2. Read directions on signs placed over faucets and fountains carefully and make sure you understand them.

3. Bring your own reusable water bottle filled with safe, clean water to school.

4. Have your blood tested for elevated lead levels to see if you need any medical treatment.

Flint pediatrician and health activist Dr. Hanna-Attisha was right about the link between elevated lead levels in water and health issues for children and others—people were testing their water, and in some cases the results were frightening. This was especially true in Newark, New Jersey, the site of another citywide water disaster. 💧

CASE STUDY: NEWARK, NEW JERSEY— THE POLITICS OF DENIAL

"Water has not contributed in any significant way to the elevated lead levels in our children's blood. Lead-based paint and dust has done that in the city of Newark, and, I would suspect, in many cities across America," said Ras Baraka, mayor of Newark, New Jersey, when he addressed the spike of high lead levels across his city with Anna Werner on *CBS This Morning* in November 2018.

Why would the mayor of Newark resist the idea of lead exposure coming from the city's aging water infrastructure, especially after the highly publicized Flint disaster? The answer is: *politics*. In May 2018, Mayor Baraka was facing a challenge from Gayle Chaneyfield Jenkins in the next mayoral election. Jenkins, a city council member, had called for action after the Natural Resources Defense Council (NRDC), a US-based international environmental organization, filed its intent in late April to sue the city over elevated lead levels in the local water supply.

"Once residents know the truth about Newark's water quality, they will be able to see for themselves that Council member Chaneyfield Jenkins is engaging in irresponsible behavior by attempting to spread falsehoods," Mayor Baraka

Reports of water crises such as the one in Newark show up frequently in the news.

said in response to his opponent's actions. But Jenkins's call for action was not a political stunt.

The situation leading up to this moment mimicked Flint's. Old water pipes had leached lead into the drinking water because the water had not been properly treated to prevent corrosion. Tests the city conducted in March 2016 exposed lead levels above 15 ppb in the water of thirty Newark public schools. The Newark school system served 35,054 students within sixty-six schools in 2016. Residents were not notified of the situation.

In May 2016, H2M Associates, a New York–based firm of architects and engineers, monitored the turbidity or water clarity in Newark. Their report described the disrepair of the infrastructure and problems with equipment maintenance and calibration. It included recommendations to update the

Pequannock Water Treatment Plant that services the city. In September 2017, the city failed to submit a requested survey of the lead service lines to the New Jersey Department of Environmental Protection. This noncompliance led the NRDC and ten other groups to call out Newark officials in a letter dated September 23, 2017, for not responding to lead contamination in the city's drinking water.

Problems continued when Newark violated the federal action level for lead for the second monitoring period, from July through December 2017. The city's consultant on the issue, Boston-based CDM Smith, informed officials that the water treatment was not effective and the pipes, like those in Flint, were corroding, leading to widespread lead contamination. Still, the city did not take action. It did not inform residents of the water crisis until October 2018.

That was when the Newark Education Workers Caucus joined with the NRDC to fight for clean, safe drinking water in the city. They decided to sue the state and city officials for the ongoing violations.

The lawsuit alleged that officials knew the methods used to stop the leaching were not working. Those officials were accused of violating the Public Notification Rule, a part of the federal Safe Drinking Water Act (1974) that requires the public to be notified if water does not meet drinking water standards.

Newark then began taking some steps toward addressing the crisis. In January 2019, Mayor Ras Baraka asked President Donald Trump for financial assistance to repair the city's infrastructure. The following month, the NRDC asked the court to mandate bottled water service to Newark families with young children and pregnant women, the two groups most impacted by lead toxicity, because filters were not helping. In the spring of 2019, other dangerous contaminants released during disinfection treatment appeared in the city's water. This signaled another problem. Could the disinfection contamination lead to Legionnaires' disease, as it did in Flint? Three city residents were diagnosed with the disease at that time.

Still, the city didn't truly come to terms with the crisis until August 2019, when the EPA instructed local officials to distribute bottled water to most of the residents of Newark. The required distribution did not include residents in the eastern Wanaque service area of the city. (The lawsuit filed by the NRDC did request bottled water for vulnerable residents in that area.)

The city's tenuous progress has been fraught with setbacks. In August 2019, a US district judge ruled that the City of Newark did not have to provide bottled water to its vulnerable residents. By October 2019, the NRDC was concerned that the city had stopped most water distribution. Erik Olson, NRDC's senior strategic director for health, wrote on the organization's blog that month: "We also are troubled that Newark still is refusing to provide filters (much less bottled water) to about 30,000 households in the Eastern part of the city who officials claim are 'unaffected' by the lead crisis." While Newark's officials claimed that these households were not affected, Newark's testing determined that dozens of homes in this part of the city had levels of lead above the EPA's action standards. The crisis continued.

The Newark Water Coalition, a frontline organization that "fights to liberate clean water as a source of life for all," was still providing cases of water for residents into March 2020, as the city continued to grapple with lead toxicity and began to face the novel coronavirus pandemic. But things were moving forward. In July 2020, the city announced that the lead levels were finally below the EPA action level. That year the city also introduced "the Newark Way of Thinking & Drinking," a program designed to educate residents about service-line replacement and ways they can reduce their lead exposure.

A major settlement was reached in January 2021 requiring the City of Newark to finish pipe replacement and ensure important health protections for city residents. "NEW [Newark Education Workers] Caucus and other residents stood up to fight for safe drinking water in Newark, securing an extraordinary victory for generations of kids who will live healthier, better lives because they won't be drinking leaded tap water," said Erik Olson in a January 26, 2021, NRDC press release. ⬧

"Everyone has a right to safe drinking water . . .
It's unfortunate that it took legal action for Newark
officials to begin to take steps to protect its most
vulnerable residents from lead, including pregnant women
and children, as lead is unsafe at any level of exposure."
—NRDC Senior Director of Health Erik Olson

Environmental Injustice Compromises Drinking Water

Water crises like those in Flint and Newark often hit areas that are already the most challenged by crime and poverty. "We're ducking and dodging bullets every day," Newark substitute teacher and parent Nafessah Venable told the *New York Times* in August 2019. "We can't even take our kids out to play. Now we've got to worry about water? Water is a necessity for life. How can we survive without clean water? It's tragic, and it's very mind-boggling to wonder what the future holds in terms of the water system."

What to Do If Your Community Has Elevated Lead Levels

1. Test your tap water.

2. Install, maintain, and use a water filter. It is important not to run hot water through your filter and to change the cartridge regularly.

3. Use only cold tap water for drinking and cooking. Don't boil water before using it. If lead is present, it will concentrate during boiling and create a higher risk of exposure.

4. Use bottled water for baby formula and baby food.

5. Test children for lead exposure.

6. If possible, replace your lead-containing pipes and fixtures.

LEAD PIPES: THE BIG PICTURE

Despite lead contamination crises like those in Flint and Newark, it's estimated that there are still more than six million lead service lines in communities throughout the United States, including many in Illinois and Ohio. These lead pipes bring water to over ten million homes in the country, according to the Environmental Defense Fund, a nonprofit US environmental advocacy group. These pipes affect everyone who uses them for their drinking water. The United States alone claims more than five hundred thousand kids with elevated lead levels. Think about how many lead pipes there are across the globe and how many more people have elevated lead levels endangering their health. The World Health Organization estimates that 240 million people in the developing world have high levels of lead in their blood. Exposure doesn't always come from lead water pipes or lead paint in old homes. In some countries, children are exposed as they work collecting and recycling batteries or from mining operations. Lots of work still needs to take place to remove lead water lines and create international standards so that a future crisis can be prevented.

Fortunately, Dr. Hanna-Attisha was right: Flint's water crisis has spurred water testing and hastened awareness of water issues in many communities. Testing helps ensure that problems can be identified and addressed earlier. On the heels of the Flint crisis, some cities, like Tucson, Arizona, began proactively removing lead piping from their infrastructure.

Although lead is a huge problem in terms of water safety, it isn't the only cause of unsafe drinking water. Toxicity can also start outside the pipes, as explored in the next few chapters. ◊

CHAPTER 2: FROM CHEMICALS TO COAL— INDUSTRIAL POLLUTION

WHEN AN INITIAL WATER SOURCE IS POLLUTED, it affects the quality of the water that eventually reaches your home. Some pollutants can't be removed through water treatment systems, and some pollutants can seep into cracked pipes between the water treatment plant and your home. Contamination of a water source often begins when industrial waste pollutes rivers, reservoirs, or underground water sources, which are called aquifers or groundwater.

Thirty-eight percent of Americans rely on groundwater for drinking. Groundwater contamination can affect those who draw their water from private wells or have municipal water, as was the case for residents of Hoosick Falls, in upstate New York.

CASE STUDY: HOOSICK FALLS, NEW YORK— POLLUTION FROM INDUSTRIAL CHEMICALS

When Flint's moms heard the news that a group of mothers in another town were facing despair and confusion over toxic drinking water, they jumped into action. Although the small upstate New York village of Hoosick Falls was almost 600 miles (965 kilometers) away, four activists from Flint, all mothers, made the journey there in October 2016. The meeting was organized partly by the New York State United Teachers and the United Teachers of Flint. The two groups of moms bonded almost instantly.

LaShaya Darisaw, one of the Flint women, shared how she and others got Flint officials to act on their behalf. "I gave 'em hell," she said. Then she recounted to the Hoosick residents how she had brought 500 people to the Flint city offices daily during the crisis. Government officials "get tired of having 500 people show up at their office . . . They have to hear you," she said.

Then it was Hoosick's turn.

Hoosick, unlike urban Flint, is a smaller community of roughly seven thousand people, including many whose families have lived there for generations. The town is dotted with farms, industry, churches, schools, and grocery stores. Stacks of wood are piled beside houses each autumn, ready for fires to warm the long winter ahead.

Hoosick Falls's water source is not a nearby river as in Flint; instead, there's groundwater in an aquifer, an underground reservoir that flows underneath local properties. About 25 percent of all rainfall in the United States seeps into the earth and becomes groundwater. This water serves as a source of fresh drinking water for 51 percent of Americans overall and 99 percent of Americans in rural areas like Hoosick Falls. About 27 trillion gallons (102 trillion liters) of groundwater are used in the United States each year for crop irrigation and drinking water. It's vital for these water sources to remain clean and plentiful. But in Hoosick Falls, they weren't.

A human-made compound called perfluorooctanoic acid, or PFOA, had made its way into the aquifer beneath the town and contaminated Hoosick's drinking water.

PFOA has been used since the 1940s to manufacture many household plastic products, such as Teflon coating, food wrappers, Gore-Tex, Scotchgard, and heat-resistant wiring. It is also used in firefighting foam. According to the US Department of Health and Human Services National Toxicology Program, PFOA has been linked to immune system disorders and cancers.

Per- and Polyfluoroalkyl Substances (PFAS)

You might hear about PFOA, PFOS, or GenX chemicals in the news. These all belong to a group of human-made chemicals called PFAS, which were developed and produced by 3M and DuPont and have been used in many types of industries since the 1940s. After the widespread and long-term use and disposal of these chemicals, they have ended up in household products and workplaces; living organisms that include fish, animals, and humans; and food and drinking water. PFAS are even in the packaging that wraps around take-out food, though some US state legislators are considering banning this use. Although US industries are no longer using PFOA and PFOS, perfluorooctane sulfonate, in manufacturing, the chemicals still come into the United States from other countries in products we use every day, like winter coats. They can also be found in some imported leather, carpets, flame-retardant clothing, packaging, nonstick cookware, and plastics. We don't know yet how our regular, daily interaction with these compounds will affect our health in the future. Since these compounds may take many human generations to break down in the environment, they are now commonly called forever chemicals. More investigation needs to be done.

THE SOURCE

The rural community of Hoosick was home to two large corporations: Saint-Gobain Performance Plastics and Honeywell.

They operated plants on McCaffrey Street in Hoosick Falls and used PFAS in their manufacturing of circuit boards, laminates, and other products. The companies released chemicals—a by-product of their industries—in waterways and on the ground in the Town of Hoosick and in southern Washington County, New York, from the 1970s to the 1990s.

The corporations didn't have permits to release PFOA in the environment. During that time period, PFOA was an unregulated contaminant, meaning the EPA didn't have specific regulations to control it. But the Clean Water Act, which recognized the importance of regulating and controlling pollution, was passed in 1972, and the Safe Water Drinking Act followed in 1974. Polluters should have been held accountable.

The PFOA leached into the ground and reached the aquifer that was the primary water source for Hoosick and Petersburgh, New York; Bennington, Vermont; and other nearby communities.

When an aquifer is contaminated, a so-called plume forms from the point of the initial contamination. The plume is a spreading pathway of pollution. Picture dropping a colored bath bomb into your bathwater. It begins to color the water around it and soon starts to spread through the entire bath. These chemicals, like the hue from a bath bomb, traveled through the aquifer underneath Hoosick and remained there for years without anyone knowing of the imminent danger. Meanwhile, everyone in Hoosick and nearby communities used the water for drinking, bathing, and cooking. Gardens were watered with it. The water bowls of Hoosick's pets were filled with it. It wasn't discolored and didn't have a

Workers drill into an aquifer to test the groundwater in the Hoosick area.

bad taste. Like the residents of Flint, no one knew the water was toxic.

THE DISCOVERY

In 2014, Michael Hickey, a Hoosick resident and former village trustee (an elected local government official), began researching the death of a local teacher. The cause of death was kidney cancer. Hickey's father, an employee of Saint-Gobain Performance Plastics for more than thirty years, had also died of kidney cancer. Was there a link between that form of cancer and PFOA levels?

Hickey suspected the local water was a factor, and he sent four samples to a lab in Canada for testing. He sent water from his own home, his mom's house, the local McDonald's, and the nearby dollar store. The report on the water samples proved his suspicions. His home water PFOA level was 540 parts per trillion (ppt). His mom's water was 460 ppt. At the time it was above the EPA advisory of 400 ppt. Since then, that advisory has been lowered to 70 ppt, making the levels of 540 and 460 extraordinarily high in comparison.

"I remember having that first conversation with the mayor," Hickey told the Albany-based *Times Union*. "He said we don't want to have a knee-jerk reaction and alarm the whole village because we've got a lot of good things going on here . . . and if we do this the water (pollution) makes it all go away."

Hoosick Falls's mayor was partly correct. These water pollution stories have a way of defining a location, but they also help make us all safer and healthier in the long run.

When Hickey's Hoosick Falls water was found to be contaminated, PFOA and PFAS, unlike lead, were not regulated chemicals. That meant that even though the EPA concluded in its 2006 Carcinogen Risk Assessment that PFOA was "likely to be carcinogenic to humans," there was still no Maximum Contaminant Level (MCL) established for PFOA. Without national EPA guidelines in 2016, it was up to each state to create regulations for chemicals in drinking water; the limit for levels of PFOA and PFAS varied among states. Vermont, which is just a few miles from Hoosick, listed advisory levels of 20 ppt. In January 2016, New York became the first US state to identify PFOA as a hazardous substance. By April the state was regulating it. By 2020, there were still no national Maximum Contaminant Levels set by the EPA for PFAS, but New York State set its levels at 10 ppt for both PFOA and PFOS that year. The process leading to New York's vote to set this level began in 2018. Michigan passed a law in July 2020 setting an even stricter level for PFOA, at 8 ppt.

THE BETRAYAL

As was the case in both Flint and Newark, local officials didn't immediately notify Hoosick Falls residents about the contaminated water supply. The contamination became part of the Hoosick Falls village record in August 2014, but EPA Regional Administrator Judith Enck indicated she wasn't notified until ten months later. In addition, the Hoosick Falls *Annual Drinking Water Quality Report for 2014* did not list any PFAS contamination.

Upon receiving the information, Enck set out to notify residents in October 2015, a full year after village officials had become aware of the problem. Water tests the following month found that Hoosick village water had a PFOA level above 400 ppt. The village's *Annual Drinking Water Quality Report for 2015* included a separate page, listing six perfluorinated compounds. Both the EPA and the New York State Department of Environmental Conservation (NYS DEC) were involved in the water and soil testing to find the extent and the source of the contamination.

Even after Enck left the EPA in 2017 and later became a Bennington College professor, she remained active in advocating for the residents of Hoosick and Petersburgh, New York, and nearby Bennington, Vermont. According to Enck, reports indicated elevated levels of PFOA in the soil and groundwater throughout the area, including the closed landfill, the Saint-Gobain manufacturing facility, and just yards away from the public water-supply wells.

Investigations into these sites and the boundaries of the poison plume in the groundwater continued.

WHAT BLOOD TESTS REVEALED

After the water in Hoosick revealed elevated PFOA levels in 2015, the New York State Department of Health tested the blood of residents there and in nearby Petersburgh to determine their levels of contamination and what action was required. This bio-monitoring program tested 2,081 people between February and April 2016. Results came back that summer.

While levels of PFOA in water are measured in parts per trillion, blood levels of the human-made compound are measured in micrograms per liter. The average level of PFOA found in blood throughout the US population is 2.1 micrograms per liter. The average level for residents who used Hoosick Falls public water was 64.2 micrograms per liter in August 2016. Similar to the lead poisoning in Flint, PFOA had entered the bodies of everyone in Hoosick Falls who drank, bathed, or cooked with the contaminated water.

Town residents remember receiving their results in June 2016. Individual letters containing test details went out to all residents, even children. Some family members recall opening those letters one by one, each revealing a different PFOA level.

Some of Hoosick's young people discovered their PFOA levels were above 120. Like the kids in Flint, these kids were frightened; they didn't know how the contamination would affect their current and future health. Some students took their letters to school, hoping their science teachers had answers for their questions about the mysterious chemical. High school chemistry teacher Brian Van Arsdale was one of those teachers. He and fellow teachers began researching PFOAs. They discovered that the risks were terrifying. There were many potentially fatal outcomes from overexposure, including kidney cancer.

"I told all my students to stop drinking the water," he said in 2016. He believed it was crucial for the students to move to bottled water instead.

The test results varied among locations as well. Some people wrongly assumed they were safe. Michelle Baker told her fourteen-year-old daughter they shouldn't worry because their water was not coming from the pipes that carried water throughout the village. Instead, it was coming from a well on their property that went deep into the groundwater under the earth. She didn't realize that all the water in Hoosick was coming from the same contaminated aquifer.

Emily Marpe thought her family home on a hill in Petersburgh was safe, but her well tested at 2100 ppt for PFOA. She received a call from the health department early one Saturday morning urging her to stop brushing her teeth "right now." Her ten-year-old daughter, Gwen, had a PFOA level in her blood of 207 micrograms per liter. It was devastating to know the water she and her family had used for four years in their new home, which she referred to as Cloud Nine, was poisoning them. "I knew I had to sell my dream house, even though we would ultimately lose all the equity we had built," she said in Congressional testimony in May 2019, at the Environment and Climate Change Subcommittee of the House Committee on Energy and Commerce.

Hoosick Falls resident Loreen Hackett's blood test came back showing her level of PFOA contamination was 266. Her grandchildren's tests also revealed high levels. The oldest child, her grandson, tested at 142 two years before in 2016. His sister's test, although lower, was still fifty times higher than the national average of 2.1.

Throughout the crisis, Hoosick residents complained about the messaging about the situation—from the individual letters indicating blood test results sent to young children to the lack of information on how to handle their health concerns.

The voices in Hoosick demanding answers echoed those of Flint's residents. The residents felt distraught and betrayed. And they wanted answers.

TAKING ACTION

Once the shock wore off, residents jumped into action. In 2016, US Senator Kirsten Gillibrand came to Hoosick High School for a village meeting. She heard the concerns of parents, students, and teachers. Dr. Susan Fenton of the Durham, North Carolina–based National Institute of Environmental Health Sciences informed everyone that the level of PFOA in a person's blood decreases by one-half every three years if, and only if, there is no additional exposure. Dr. Fenton advised residents to be vigilant about water filtration, and community members, including students, spoke up.

"It's not just a physical crisis degrading our bodies in ways that we cannot guess, but it's a mental crisis as well. For the rest of our lives, Hoosick Falls and Petersburgh residents will live in fear—fear of what is to come, fear of what has already been done, and fear that our lives will never return to how they used to be."
—Anna Wysocki, a young Hoosick resident speaking at a town meeting in July 2016, soon after she graduated from high school

"Why won't you stop poisoning our children?" Loreen Hackett pleaded at a New York State Senate hearing. She was just one of the residents who took Hoosick's message to lawmakers, sharing her family's heart-wrenching experiences. She and many other New York women became the unofficial voices of Hoosick's water crisis. Like so many mothers and grand-mothers affected by water contamination throughout the country, Loreen was on a mission to protect future generations.

These upstate residents joined with the National PFAS Contamination Community Coalition to support and advocate for one another and for all of us. By 2020, there were twenty US community groups in the coalition, representing regions that had been poisoned by these chemicals. There were over fifteen hundred contamination sites that ranged from Alaska to Colorado, from Michigan to North Carolina, from Massachusetts to New Hampshire. And it's not just the United States that has been at risk—there are toxic water sites worldwide.

These community groups continue to speak out and raise their voices, advocating for legislation, health monitoring, and cleanup. And their voices are being heard.

In the summer of 2017, Hoosick Falls was designated an EPA "superfund" site. This designation identified the site as a risk to human health and a candidate for priority cleanup. By that December, Hoosick schools and the New York State Department of Conservation had set up a proactive mainte-nance schedule for the schools' water filtration systems. River pollution can often be "cleaned up" by dredging the river for the settled pollutants, whereas groundwater pollution is not as easily remedied. The process is much more costly and requires pumping out the water, treating it, and then returning it to the underground reservoir or, if that isn't feasible, leav-ing it to reduce naturally, which can take years. While the EPA and NYS DEC worked on remedying the contamination, res-idents received water filters to protect them from ingesting additional toxic water.

Although Hoosick residents received filters, they were instructed to remain vigilant about any future exposure to PFOA, as Dr. Fenton had advised—from local water as well as from household items such as nonstick cookware. In addition to exposure from household products and clothing, the residents were also still living with toxic groundwater underneath the village.

In a December 2018 speech, New York governor Andrew Cuomo said, "There is a growing water crisis in our state . . . New York must stand up, take the lead to clean our water for our children and our children's children." He added, "Do the science, regulate the chemicals and leave the planet better than we found it."

Shortly after that speech, the New York State Drinking Water Quality Council met. It agreed to recommend setting the state's Maximum Contaminant Levels for PFOA and PFOS at 10 parts per trillion. ◊

Erin Brockovich in Hoosick

In the 1990s, Erin Brockovich, a consumer advocate and environmental activist, helped build a lawsuit against Pacific Gas and Electric for contaminating water in the town of Hinkley, California, with hexavalent chromium, a carcinogen. The chemical, used to suppress rust formation, had seeped into the town's groundwater. The case garnered nationwide attention and was the subject of a 2000 movie starring Julia Roberts.

Brockovich demonstrated her continued effort to champion clean water on a visit to Hoosick in January 2016. "It doesn't matter what your political party is. It doesn't matter what the color of your skin is. It doesn't matter if you're rich or poor. Everyone is entitled to have safe and pure water available to them and their families at all times," she said to the gathered crowd.

FEDERAL ACTION ON PFAS

While the New York State regulation was a step forward for Hoosick, regulation of PFAS is still needed at the national level.

Before the EPA can set a limit for any PFAS compounds in drinking water, it has to go through a formal process to declare its intent.

By early 2021, there was still no national regulation for PFAS. Even when regulations and protections are put in place for our water safety, ongoing effort to defend them is required because they can be removed with the stroke of a pen. Each new White House administration can authorize deregulations as it sees fit. When it comes to regulations and protections, sometimes it feels like one step forward, two steps back. That's why it's important that we continue to insist that our health be protected and make our voices heard.

COAL COUNTRY

While Hoosick's toxic water came from a manufacturing plant, other communities throughout the United States—including many rural communities—face industrial contamination from a different source: the coal industry.

The process of extracting coal is hazardous for miners, who breathe in harmful coal dust every day, but the contamination doesn't stop there. For every facet of the industry—from extraction to burning—coal affects the drinking water of the people living in the mining region, those near the coal-fired plants, and the broader society.

Let's begin with an overview of extraction.

Extraction

Coal is a fossil fuel. It is the remains of prehistoric animals and plants that lived in bogs and swamps. Over millions of years these remains transformed into a combustible black rock. Although coal is burned in fewer and fewer US power plants as the country moves toward greener energy solutions, it is still mined, or extracted, in many areas.

There are two ways to mine coal. The first is to dig for it. This process, which involves creating deep underground tunnels, can have long-lasting effects on many bodies of water, including aquifers. When some substances in the ground are exposed to air and water through the mining process, a chemical reaction occurs. Pyrite (an iron sulfide), for example, reacts with water to create iron and sulfuric acid. The highly acidic water causes acid mine drainage. It dissolves other heavy metals, such as copper and lead, and chemical elements such as arsenic and carries them downstream. These harmful substances drain out of the mining site and into creeks, streams, ponds, and rivers. If the acid mine drainage contains iron, the iron may precipitate (drop) out of the water to the riverbed, turning it red, yellow, or orange.

Drainage of pollutants from coal mines (and other mining, including for uranium and iron) occurs for years, even after a mine is abandoned. It is the primary pollutant of surface water in the mid-Atlantic region of the United States, leading to the degradation of more than 4,500 miles (7,242 kilometers) of streams. The EPA monitors pollution sites, including over forty-eight abandoned coal mines in the United States, all of which pose a threat of leaching heavy metals like mercury, cadmium, and lead into our waterways.

The second type of coal mining, mountaintop removal, is practiced mostly in Appalachia. It involves clearcutting forests, then either burning the debris or dumping it into valleys. To reach the coal beneath, millions of pounds of explosives are used to blow off the top layer of the mountains. The debris left behind from the clearcutting, the explosions, and the digging often washes into the streams below.

After extraction by either method, the coal is washed with water and chemicals before it is transported to power plants and other consumers for burning. The washing process creates coal slurry, which consists of water, coal dust, and clay—and often includes toxic materials such as arsenic, lead, chromium, and mercury. The slurry is then piped into storage ponds. Sometimes, coal slurry ponds spill into nearby waterways, contaminating drinking water supplies. That's what happened in Martin County, Kentucky, in October 2000.

CASE STUDY: MARTIN COUNTY, KENTUCKY— COAL SLURRY CONTAMINATION

A small drip of water trickled from a crack in a cliff along a four-lane highway in rural Martin County, Kentucky. Resident Jasper Davis tilted his plastic bottle under the black piping rigged to catch the fresh spring water.

"Tastes better than what the city water does," he said in October 2019. "Way better."

Davis isn't the only one who used this spring. Many other locals visited it often to replenish their drinking water. Even on cold days, when the temperature of the air was just above freezing, Martin County resident Hope Workman filled jugs with the cool, clear spring water, as she had for the past twenty years.

Gathering water at this Martin County spring was a necessity for many people in the mountain community bordering West Virginia. Water problems have plagued the county for decades, including a massive coal slurry spill in 2000 that polluted the source of the county's drinking water. The slurry sent roughly 306 million gallons (1.2 billion liters) of toxic waste containing arsenic, lead, and mercury into two tributaries of the Tug Fork River. Jasper Davis remembers how horrible it was. It poisoned the water and killed all the fish in the creek near his home.

The Martin County coal slurry spill at Wolf Creek in 2000.

Water contamination issues persisted for years. In 2017, customers of the public water system received bills with notices on the back stating that the levels of trihalomethanes and haloacetic acids were above federal limits.

Further complicating the situation, the county faced serious infrastructure issues. The 300 miles (483 kilometers) of piping that's used to move water across the county is susceptible to leaking. The system is so bad that half the water leaving the Martin County Water District treatment plant doesn't even make it to the faucets of county residents. Because of those leaks, debris and chemical residue from the mining industry enter the water system.

And in addition to all the pollution problems, county residents suffered from high water bills. The EPA indicates that those bills shouldn't cost more than 2.5 percent of a household's income, yet one in ten US households cannot afford their water bills. In 2018, the water rates in Martin County increased by 41 percent. As a result, the Public Service Commission of Kentucky ordered an outside management company to take over the district, and some of the increase was designed to offset the cost of that change in management and the repair of waterlines.

So it's no surprise that, like Jasper Davis, many Martin County residents turn to the spring for their water. "Water rates so high, they just come out here to get the spring water because it's safer to drink and cook in," said Davis. ◖

Burning Coal

Acid mine drainage and coal slurry are toxic enough, but they are not the only hazardous results of coal mining. Once the coal is washed, it is burned to create energy. The burning leaves behind a substance called coal ash. This gray powder contains toxic compounds, like mercury, lead, and arsenic. Like the slurry, it is toxic to all living organisms. According to the EPA, coal ash is one of the most abundant types of industrial waste produced in the United States. The Union for Concerned Scientists states that more than one hundred million tons of coal ash and other waste products are generated by coal-fired power plants every year. Nearly 130 million tons were generated in 2014.

Most of that waste is stored in unlined ponds or pits and has the potential to leach into waterways and contaminate drinking water. A 2019 study by the Environmental Integrity Project and Earthjustice, among other organizations, reported that coal ash is contaminating the groundwater beneath 91 percent of coal plants in the United States.

Coal-fired power plants also contaminate thousands of miles of rivers and streams. They dump water laced with dangerous pollutants, such as arsenic, lead, and mercury, into waterways. The Town of Pines, Indiana, was declared an EPA Superfund site in 2004 after Northern Indiana Public Service Company sidestepped regulations by dumping coal ash into unlined landfills where waste can leach out. It also used the waste in roadway construction sites, where poisonous runoff flowed into waterways. Making matters worse, the water used to run the plants must come from a nearby body of water, which can deplete local water supplies and damage wetlands.

There are many stories of how the coal industry has had an impact on water supplies, including a 2008 spill that occurred when a retaining wall around Tennessee's Kingston Fossil Plant collapsed. It released more than 1 billion gallons (3.78 billion liters) of toxic sludge into nearby rivers. Year after year, stories fill our news feeds. And in 2014, another one made national news—in Dan River, North Carolina—and affected people in two states.

CASE STUDY: THE DAN RIVER, NORTH CAROLINA— COAL ASH CONTAMINATION

On Super Bowl Sunday in February 2014, while people were getting together to celebrate football, a drainage pipe ruptured under a coal ash pond at the Duke Energy Dan River Steam Station in Eden, North Carolina, sending thirty-nine thousand tons of coal ash into North Carolina's Dan River.

The river is used as a source of drinking water for residents and livestock in North Carolina and Virginia as well as for crop irrigation. The river's watershed is home to wildlife, including two endangered species—the Roanoke logperch and the James spinymussel. Residents in North Carolina and Virginia canoe and kayak in the river.

The spilled coal ash contained toxic substances, including arsenic, cadmium, copper, lead, mercury, nickel, and unburned carbon. It coated the river bottom with toxic ash for 70 miles (112.6 kilometers) downstream, rendering the river polluted and unusable.

Duke Energy was sued in 2014 by the federal, North Carolina, and Virginia governments for environmental damage from the leak that caused the disaster. The company agreed in a settlement with the EPA to pay $3 million for cleanup. This settlement required Duke Energy to locate the coal ash deposits along the Dan River and remove them. The cleanup process took over five years.

You'd think that the cleanup would mark the end of the problems, but coal ash spills cause additional long-term risks. Ten years after the Kingston spill in Tennessee, for instance, workers involved in the cleanup suffered from ailments linked to the toxic ash they'd carried home on their clothes.

"We know coal ash and substances like arsenic do not go away, they don't disappear, they don't evaporate," said Frank Holleman, senior attorney with the Southern Environmental Law Center, which sued Duke Energy over its coal ash handling on behalf of various groups.

The Dan River spill was the third-largest coal ash spill in US history, and it led to a new state law requiring all coal ash storage ponds to be closed by 2029. ◊

How to Clean a River

To clean up the Dan River, Duke Energy used a gigantic underwater vacuum that fit atop a barge. The first step was to stir up the top layer of ash that had settled on the river floor and suck up the cloud that formed. The next step was to screen out the larger debris. The remaining river water was cleaned of fine particles, and the clean water was deposited back in the river. The waste that was retrieved was hauled away to a landfill.

A Short-Lived EPA Ruling

To the relief of many coal country activists, the EPA issued a rule in 2015 about coal combustion residuals (CCR)—coal ash, fly ash, boiler slag, and bottom ash—that are generated by coal-fired power plants. Groundwater near coal ash ponds would be tested, and standards would be set for pond construction. Coal companies would have to clean up any damage from their plant wastewater leaks by 2018. It was a great cause for hope. It had taken the EPA four years of research to create the standards, which marked the first update linked to coal plant wastewater discharge in thirty years.

This rule was bound to change our lives. It would eliminate an estimated 1.4 billion pounds of toxic pollutants from being released into waterways each year.

But the hope—and the ruling—was short-lived.

Every administration that comes into power in the United States can change laws and regulations. It didn't take long for President Donald Trump's EPA administrators—Scott Pruitt and then Andrew Wheeler—to slash the protections that the previous administration had enacted. The clean water ruling ended up being dismantled—a boost for coal corporations. The regulations loosened, and the 2018 deadline for cleanup was extended to 2020. This meant communities with polluted water would have to wait two years longer for cleaning.

The Impact of Plants Closing

Despite the regulation rollbacks, many coal plants have closed in recent years as the United States moves away from fossil fuels and toward greener energy alternatives. There were at least 289 closures between 2010 and 2020, including 50 in the first two years of President Trump's administration. The release of toxic debris has decreased accordingly. Duke Energy's Dan River plant was replaced in 2012 by a natural gas-fired plant, and as of 2019, at least half of Duke Energy's coal-fired plants in North Carolina had been decommissioned. In addition, the Tennessee Valley Authority coal-fired plant at Paradise Fossil Plant in Drakesboro, Kentucky closed in 2020.

While closing or converting old coal-fired plants and coal mines decreases the emission of greenhouse gases, provides us with cleaner air, and decreases the toxic spread of contaminants into our water supplies, there is another side to the story. The closures cause economic hardship for the people who have been employed by the coal industry for generations. In communities like Martin County, Kentucky, everyone feels the impact—from surface miners to gas station clerks.

Since July 2010, employment in Martin County has fallen 32 percent. Coal mining is costly and labor intensive. As the numbers of coal-fired plants close, miners find themselves out of work. The closures also represent a significant loss of revenue from a coal severance tax for the county, which hampered expensive infrastructure repairs needed to provide fresh, clean water to the Kentucky communities impacted. The median income in the county is $29,054, with 56 percent of households in 2016 without workers drawing an income.

The economics forced the Martin County water board to raise rates and send disconnect letters to three hundred residences for lack of payment. The increased water rates pushed residents to the brink. One man was accused of stealing water and arrested.

In good news, out-of-work coal workers are now finding jobs in the solar power industry. Edelen Renewables announced the development of a solar power farm on a former coal mine in December of 2020 that will put roughly 300 people to work in the county. Martin County will see a transformation from coal to solar.

Moving from Coal to Natural Gas

While some areas are moving from coal to solar, others are moving from coal to natural gas. The move away from coal has been hastened by many factors, including the growth of fracking—the process of drawing petroleum resources, including oil and natural gas, out of the earth. But natural gas also brings its share of concerns. And there is another facet of energy production that warrants exploration— transportation. Oil and gas are transported around the world through pipelines that pose a threat of leaking into our waterways. As more and more of those pipelines develop leaks, more and more people are protesting their installation across their land and underneath their rivers. ◗

CHAPTER 3: PIPELINES AND PROTESTS— FRACKING CONTAMINATION

THE FOSSIL FUEL ENERGY THAT POWERS our cars, lights our world, and cools and heats our homes has a price that goes deeper than the energy bill your family pays, and the price is always tied to water in some way. As is the case with coal, there are significant hidden costs linked to natural gas, another fossil fuel.

To use natural gas as an energy source, it must first be extracted from beneath the earth's surface. The process of extraction is a method of drilling called hydraulic fracturing—or fracking—and it was invented by the Halliburton company in 1949.

The first step is withdrawing groundwater or surface water and mixing it with additives to create fracking liquids. These added chemicals are kept secret and unregulated by the extraction companies. (This is known as the Halliburton Loophole because Vice President Dick Cheney, a former Halliburton chief executive, removed the EPA's authority to regulate this process in the 2005 Energy Policy Act.)

The fracking liquid is then injected into underground rock using a high-pressure drill, which fractures the rock and releases natural gas. Wastewater, or flowback, returns to the surface. It should be disposed of or reused, but because this process isn't regulated, it often ends up in our waterways. Fracking chemicals seep into the ground and pollute aquifers or are injected directly into groundwater resources. Sometimes, they are even sprayed on dusty, dry roads.

While the state issues permits to drill, the oil and gas company must also obtain the rights to drill into the land—which is often privately owned—before fracking can begin. Corporate representatives from the oil and gas companies go door-to-door, making offers to landowners.

That's what happened in Bradford County, Pennsylvania.

CASE STUDY: BRADFORD COUNTY, PENNSYLVANIA— FRACKING FLUIDS LEAK

Carol French was one of the Bradford County, Pennsylvania, residents who got a knock on the door in 2006 from East Resources offering her money to drill on her farm. She agreed to a five-year lease, which was then sold to Chesapeake Energy Corporation.

Charlie Clark also got a knock on his door. He felt like he had won the lottery when he was offered roughly $10,000 per month to allow drilling for two gas wells on his dairy farm by Chief Oil & Gas. The money would keep arriving as long as there was revenue from the sale of the gas. It was easy to see how the extra income might help a struggling family farm. Barns could be built. New tractors could be bought. College funds could be started for kids. A much-needed vacation could be planned. Charlie accepted the offer.

Not only did the companies offer money to Bradford County residents for their mineral rights, but they also promised jobs—from construction to security positions—at the drilling sites.

And so farmer after farmer put pen to paper to sign away mineral rights. If they didn't do so, they were likely to experience some pressure. At a presentation at Pennsylvania State University, Chesapeake Energy representatives spoke to local farmers who hadn't leased their land, claiming it was each farmer's patriotic duty to "assure our Country would be independent from foreign oil."

Once rights were obtained, construction began—first roads leading through the farmland to the drilling sites, and then pouring cement well pads and preparing the sites for drilling. The fracking operation was underway.

But Carol French and her Bradford County neighbors did not see better times after they signed their agreements. Their agricultural land turned industrial as trucks rumbled along new roads, and by 2009, reports of contaminated household wells sprung up across the drilled Pennsylvania farms.

Still, drilling continued. In the winter of 2010, three fracking wells were drilled near Carol's dairy farm. In the summer of 2011, drilling commenced on five more wells nearby. ◊

CONTAMINATION

In May 2011, the Pennsylvania Department of Environmental Protection (DEP) fined Chesapeake Energy $900,000 for causing the contamination of sixteen water wells by fracking waste products in Bradford County and another $188,000 for a fire that injured workers. The contamination fine was the most substantial single penalty the DEP had ever levied against an oil and gas company. It was meant to send a strong message. In addition to the fine, Chesapeake Energy agreed to pay for water treatment.

The contamination problem wasn't only with the drilling companies, though—it also involved treatment facilities that were releasing partially treated wastewater into rivers. The DEP asked the drilling companies to voluntarily stop delivering waste liquids to those facilities.

Earlier, in April of that year, while Chesapeake Energy was fighting the fine in court, a blowout occurred at one of the fracking sites. It leaked thousands of gallons of hydraulic fracturing fluid onto nearby fields and a creek. Chesapeake Energy suspended the completion of wells in the area, but only for three weeks.

As it turned out, the fines didn't put an end to the problems on local farms. By the spring of 2012, Carol French's pond water had turned "white, with a green moss settling on top of the sand." She claimed the consistency of the water was like gelatin.

By October of that year, Carol's daughter became very sick. Her liver, spleen, and ovaries were all enlarged. Carol moved her out of state, away from what she believed was making her ill—the water. Then her neighbors began to get sick.

TAKING ACTION

In 2008, years before her daughter became sick, Carol and fellow dairy farmer Carolyn Knapp, also from Bradford County, founded the Pennsylvania Landowner Group for Awareness and Solutions. The group would share the impact of fracking on their land, which includes the contamination of farm produce, livestock, and water. Like residents in communities facing poisoning from PFAS and lead, they joined together to raise awareness and seek justice.

"We have documentation from DEP that fracking and drilling has contaminated our water," Carol told North Carolina residents who were considering leasing their land in 2011. "What we are seeing is that people are first losing their water, and then they find out that their children are becoming sick." She explained how people moved away from their homes and temporarily rented places to live in areas away from the contaminated water. But the cost of rent, in addition to the mortgage on their home, exhausted their finances.

It has taken years to resolve the issues around fracking in Pennsylvania. In 2020, the state's Department of Health declared that it was taking steps to learn more about health risks linked to fracking. This followed criticism after a grand jury found that the DEP "did not take sufficient action in response to the fracking boom" ten years earlier to protect residents from the industry's damaging impact on health. The deputy secretary of the DEP's Office of Oil and Gas Management, Scott Perry, challenged the grand jury's claims, citing an improper question on the complaint form and other irregularities. The grand jury listened to the testimony of many people, including thirty current and former DEP employees and seventy-five families, to inform their conclusions and recommendations. Suggestions for addressing the fracking problems included disclosing the chemicals used in the process, making transportation of toxic waste safer, and affording the state's attorney general's office criminal jurisdiction over the oil and gas companies.

But while testimony was given and a grand jury stated its recommendations, residents in Bradford County were still living with new wells being drilled and older sites being "refreshed," meaning they were being refracked. "I'm living in limbo," said Carolyn Knapp in January 2021. "You don't know when it is going to surface." The *it* referred to the unhealthy change in her water. While her farm's leases have expired and no wells were drilled, the impact on her water by other fracking wells in the area was still a possibility. Her cows were able to sense the fracking before her. They stopped drinking the water and opted instead to slurp from muddy puddles on certain days. "Cows are very sensitive to it," she said.

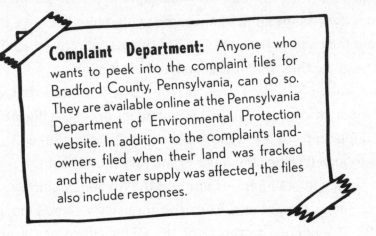

Complaint Department: Anyone who wants to peek into the complaint files for Bradford County, Pennsylvania, can do so. They are available online at the Pennsylvania Department of Environmental Protection website. In addition to the complaints land-owners filed when their land was fracked and their water supply was affected, the files also include responses.

EVIDENCE

Although the EPA found evidence in a 2016 study that fracking has contributed to drinking water contamination, Congress has yet to do away with the Halliburton loophole. In February 2017, H.R. 1068 was introduced in the House to amend the Safe Drinking Water Act; the intent was to repeal the exemption for hydraulic fracturing set up in the Halliburton loophole. As of June 2021 it had yet to be passed.

In the meantime, fracking continues, and not just in Pennsylvania. To the west in Colorado, drilling sites dot the prairie landscape. Oil and gas corporations, facing little regulation and big profits, work to obtain drilling rights and compete with other extraction companies for a finite amount of natural gas in the state's ground. Meanwhile, industry television commercials strive to convince property owners that selling mineral rights will benefit them and local economies.

CASE STUDY: BELLA ROMERO ACADEMY, GREELEY, COLORADO—KIDS IN THE CROSSFIRE

The commercial flashed across the screen on the Colorado television station. It depicted a young, white, blond teacher named Sarah. She addressed the viewers directly: "I was born and raised in Colorado. My parents were born and raised here as well. My mom and dad and my brother are all in the oil and gas industry. The industry gives so much back to our community. My husband's the head football coach here, and they donated money for our brand-new, state-of-the-art training rooms. They're present; they truly care about our community and the schools and the parks and the people in our town, in general. When they donate things to our community, it makes it feel like we're all in this together." As the spot ended, the logo for PDC Energy flashed on the screen.

COLORADO'S MULTIBILLION-DOLLAR INDUSTRY

PDC Energy is one of about fifty extraction companies based in Colorado. Their messaging, as highlighted in the aforementioned commercial, is part of the ongoing conversation about fracking. How viewers perceive the message depends on their own bias. Proponents look favorably on the money donated by these companies to schools and communities. Others regard commercials like this as propaganda from corporations that might not have their best interests in mind. No matter what the viewer's perspective may be, it is essential to weigh the companies' messaging against the health risks that accompany the extraction practices. Information is vital to drawing informed conclusions.

Extraction Oil & Gas, another Colorado extraction company with operations in the Greater Wattenberg Field of the state's Denver-Julesburg Basin, is one of the top ten extractors in Weld County, Colorado. According to the Weld County government web page, there are just over twenty thousand active wells in the county. Between 2013 and July 2019, Extraction Oil & Gas extracted 8.6 billion cubic feet of natural gas through fracking from its sites. But what launched Extraction Oil & Gas into the public spotlight wasn't the amount of natural gas it extracted but rather *where* it fracked.

ON THE OTHER SIDE OF THE FENCE

In 2019, Patricia Nelson stood in the parking lot of Bella Romero Academy, a K–8 school in the town of Greeley in Weld County, Colorado, with her son, second grader Diego. She had grown up just a mile away, left home, got married, and returned to raise her son in Greeley near the grasslands, mountains, and family of her own childhood. She was amazed to find the amount of fracking underway in the area when she returned. Looking over her shoulder that day in the parking lot, she saw—not far from the chain-link fence of the school's play yards—a fracking pad with at least six wells and flowback containment cylinders. It was the work of Extraction Oil & Gas.

The drilling site wasn't originally planned to be located there. It was only after meeting with widespread opposition from parents and neighbors of Frontier Charter Academy, also in the Greeley-Evans School District 6, about drilling near that school, that Extraction Oil & Gas moved its drilling plan close to Bella Romero.

In 2016, when it filed a new application to drill near the small brick school, the company insisted that the site's

Patricia Nelson became the voice for her son and the other students impacted by fracking near the Bella Romero school.

relocation had nothing to do with the pressure from the Frontier Charter Academy community. But the two schools, although in the same district, were vastly different. Frontier's student body consisted of 77 percent white middle-class children. Bella Romero had a much different student body—mostly an immigrant and refugee community that was 87 percent students of color, with 90 percent of the students receiving free or reduced lunches. Also, few parents of Bella Romero students spoke English as a first language, causing many to have difficulty deciphering the legal language of the permits and proceedings linked to the extraction plan nearby. As the Bella Romero situation demonstrates, it's often these communities who are hardest hit by environmental challenges.

Nelson's voice cracked in the school's parking lot in 2019. "This project endangers the students of Bella Romero, the community, and the state of Colorado." She took a breath. "This is setting a dangerous precedent—industry has been allowed to encroach on our open spaces, our homes, and now our schools. They are robbing my child and his classmates of the high quality of life that Coloradans have enjoyed for generations."

Having a drilling site so close to the school posed many potential problems. Other drilling sites, operated by the same company, had suffered explosions that killed workers. Bella Romero needed an evacuation plan in case such an event happened just a few hundred feet from the school. Few sidewalks and the neighborhood's layout made a quick evacuation challenging, however.

Nelson also worried about the health risks the operation posed, including air pollution from methane and other chemicals as well as the possibility of the water around the drilling site being contaminated by fracking waste. Fracking sites have been linked to higher risks of cancer, developmental delays, premature births, and other health issues. A 2016 study conducted by the Johns Hopkins Bloomberg School of Public Health also found a link between fracking and increases in mild, moderate, and severe cases of asthma.

There were other issues as well: Living near a fracking site, with all its noise, light, vibrations, and truck traffic, can disturb sleep, lower home values, and—in the case of the school—adversely affect learning.

Unlike many Bella Romero parents, Nelson had the means to withdraw her son, Diego, from the school, but she was determined to fight for the families that couldn't. And she was mostly fighting alone. The issue wasn't that Bella Romero's parents don't care about their children—they do. But extraction companies employ roughly nineteen thousand residents, including many from Bella Romero families. Extraction Oil & Gas pays some of the highest salaries in Weld County. Where would those residents work if they weren't working for the oil and gas industry? In addition, there are many undocumented families in the county. Some did not want to put themselves and their families in jeopardy of being deported by speaking out about the fracking situation. Not many wanted to rock the boat.

But Patricia Nelson disrupted the status quo to protect Bella Romero's students. In April 2017, she joined a lawsuit to fight the nearby fracking operation. As for other communities where oil and gas companies employ many residents, the situation in Greeley became an issue of conflicting loyalties.

But Nelson had rallied allies to her cause.

"The harms fracking does to nearby communities are well-documented, and it is irresponsible to allow drilling to occur next to where children learn and play before a ruling, as in this case, can be issued. We urge the court to recognize the irreparable harm these children are being faced with and put a stop to this dirty, dangerous project immediately." —Eric Huber, Sierra Club managing attorney, April 2019

PROTESTS AND PUBLIC PRESSURE

As part of its mission to combat environmental injustice, the Sierra Club joined in the lawsuit in 2017 that Patricia Nelson and other Bella Romero parents were bringing against the oil company. Their involvement brought more national attention—and public pressure—to the situation.

Local protesters also took action to draw attention to the fracking operation. Cullen Lobe, a Colorado State University

Teen activist Cullen Lobe became instrumental in the fight against fracking near the Colorado elementary school.

graduate who studied journalism and environmental affairs, was part of a group that held peaceful rallies almost every day to make their voices heard against what they felt was a war against the land and the people living there.

One morning in March 2018, in the midst of a court battle to stop the drilling, Lobe and a handful of other activists arrived at the drilling site and found the young children on the playground in tears. The children were stressed and upset at the heightened activity going on near their school. Lobe and the other protesters peacefully approached the worker operating a bulldozer and asked him to leave. He didn't. The group then chained one of the protesters to the bulldozer, obstructing it. Minutes later, plainclothes police officers arrived. Lobe was arrested.

According to Nelson, Lobe's actions had an impact. "I

really think that Cullen's lockdown did shine some light, at least made some noise," she recalled later.

The attention led Extraction Oil & Gas to agree to curtail fracking during the school year and limit its activity to times when the school was not officially in session, such as vacation periods.

It was a small community-led win, but large-scale regulation was still needed. Two years earlier, despite statewide protests, the Colorado Supreme Court eliminated municipal fracking bans, claiming that the state's power to regulate the industry trumped local legislation. This ruling meant that local communities could not ban fracking within their borders. One Colorado city, Longmont, reached into its coffers to pay $3 million to two fracking companies to pack up and leave the area in 2018. Not all communities, however, have the resources to do that. If they can't place a ban or pay to remove fracking companies, these communities must deal with the impact and the risks of fracking.

The situation for Longmont changed in July 2020. The Colorado Oil and Gas Conservation Commission (COGCC) reversed a decision to join a lawsuit filed by oil and gas companies against the city of Longmont. This was the second lawsuit by the state against the city's fracking limits. This meant that the state of Colorado was overriding the decision by the community to set limits on fracking, which was seen as an assault against the democratic process.

But there was also good news for activists later that year when the COGCC approved a 2,000-foot (610-meter) setback rule. New oil and gas drilling sites now had to be placed this distance away from homes, schools, and other protected areas. The previous rule allowed drilling sites to come within

500 feet (152 meters) of homes and 1,000 feet (304 meters) of schools like Bella Romero.

In 2021, Greeley activists rose up again in their quest to protect their water, this time speaking out against a plan to switch their current water source from the Poudre River mountain water to the Terry Ranch Aquifer in northwest Weld County. Save Greeley's Water, an activist group including engineers, scientists, residents, environmentalists, and water professionals, argued that water in the aquifer was laced with mining contaminants, including uranium. While the city acknowledged claims of uranium in the water, it also promised the water would be cleaned to healthy standards. The City of Greeley saw Terry Ranch as a way forward that would provide the area with aquifer storage and recovery that would counter any drought. As we can see, in an area of mineral and resource extraction, water issues are ever present. 💧

FROM EXTRACTION TO TRANSPORTATION

Close to eighteen million Americans live within one mile (1.6 kilometers) of oil and gas wells. Although several states, including Vermont, Maryland, New York, and Washington, have a moratorium on fracking, the industry is still expected to increase nationwide. Many communities are facing or will face the same risks as the residents of Greeley, Colorado.

And the risks don't end with extraction. After extraction, oil and gas have to be transported. Oil is sent through pipelines to refineries and then on to power plants, or it is loaded onto ships bound for other countries. High pressure is used to transport gas through interstate pipelines to consumers.

As with extraction, there is a steep price attached to oil and gas transportation, which includes hazardous spills and deadly explosions. Pipelines can be dangerous. That's why, from April 2016 to February 2017, thousands of voices were raised to protest the Dakota Access Pipeline (DAPL) that threatened the drinking water of the Standing Rock Sioux Reservation, which straddles the border between North and South Dakota.

CASE STUDY: THE STANDING ROCK SIOUX RESERVATION, NORTH AND SOUTH DAKOTA—PIPELINE PROTESTS BECOME A MOVEMENT

The Standing Rock Sioux Reservation is home to bands of the Dakota and Lakota Nations—about sixteen thousand enrolled tribal members in total on approximately 841,700 acres (340,624 hectares) of land. The ancestors of these Indigenous people once lived and governed in what are now the Dakotas, Montana, Wyoming, Minnesota, Iowa, and Nebraska. They lived on this land for thousands of years, long before the United States was formed. Standing Rock is the birthplace of the famous Hunkpapa Lakota chief and holy man Sitting Bull, known in his language as Tatanka Iyotake.

The reservation, established in 1868, is now much smaller than the tribe's original homeland. It's even smaller than it was in the original treaty that created the reservation. Over the years, Congress reduced the reservation land, dividing it into smaller separate reservations, including today's Standing Rock Sioux Reservation that now lies solely in North and South Dakota.

The Missouri River is the reservation's primary water source.

"We are governed by prayer . . .
We are Mother Earth defending herself."
—Cedric Goodhouse, Hunkpapa Lakota chairman
of the Standing Rock Sioux Reservation

THE PIPELINE THREAT

In 2015, the US Army Corps of Engineers (USACE), which is the federal body in charge of the country's waterways, sent a letter to the Tribal Historic Preservation Office to begin a permitting process for a 1,172-mile (1,887-kilometer) crude oil pipeline. The route for the Dakota Access Pipeline would begin in the shale oil fields in northwest North Dakota and travel through South Dakota and Iowa, and end near Patoka, Illinois. The oil would then be transported to Texas, where it would be sold and shipped around the world. As part of its route, the pipeline, owned by Energy Transfer Partners, parent company of Dakota Access LLC, would cross under the Missouri River, just a half mile from Standing Rock Sioux Reservation. If the pipe leaked in that stretch, it could poison the reservation's drinking water.

Legally, the US Army Corps of Engineers is required to consult with tribes on any potential impact that construction would cause, but the tribe's requests for investigations and impact reports by the USACE went unanswered.

Other government agencies, including the EPA and the US Department of the Interior, voiced their concerns in 2016 for the people in the area and the impact on their water quality should even the slightest leak or spill occur.

Still, the plans proceeded. The USACE issued a final fast-track regulatory review known as the Nationwide Permit for construction without requiring the energy corporation to go through the lengthier, more thorough permitting application period. This shorter reviewing process allowed Dakota Access to continue construction using its conclusion in the 2015 *Draft Environmental Assessment* that the proposed project was "not expected to have any significant, direct, indirect, or cumulative impacts on the environment."

Authorized USACE district commanders for the Omaha, Nebraska; Saint Louis, Missouri; and Rock Island, Illinois, districts signed the Nationwide Permit in July 2016. The USACE approved approximately two hundred water crossings for the pipeline and indicated that an Environmental Impact Study prepared under the National Environmental Policy Act of 1969 was not required for any parts of the pipeline under the USACE jurisdiction.

The Standing Rock Sioux (Hunkpapa Oyate) filed an injunction (a legal order) in July 2016 to curtail the fast-track permit and require more studies on the pipeline's impact. This was followed by countersuits from Dakota Access.

What could the tribe do to protect its water? Members had already taken legal steps to stop the construction, without success. So they began to raise their voices.

VOICES RAISED

Indigenous teens, who raised awareness of the pipeline threat through social media, fueled the protests. Tokata Iron Eyes and her friends created the #NoDAPL hashtag that trended around the world. Soon, Twitter was filled with the hashtags #StandingRock and #NoDAPL along with photos of groups of Indigenous people standing out in the cold, teepees and other tents pitched, banners waving. The opponents gathered in 2016 to form what became known as the Oceti Sakowin camp. Behind those hashtags and photos was a fight for clean water and Indigenous rights that was beginning to spread worldwide.

The 2016 youth effort to raise awareness didn't stop there. Young Indigenous and non-Indigenous youths ran 500 miles (805 kilometers) to show their opposition to the pipeline—departing Cannonball, North Dakota, on April 24 and arriving on May 3 at the district office of the US Army Corps of Engineers in Omaha, Nebraska. But the pipeline wasn't stopped. So they continued their effort. On July 26, 2016, members of the group, including twelve-year-old Alice Brown Otter and Bobbi Jean Three Legs, a young mother in her early twenties, began to run 2,000 miles (3,219 kilometers) from the Standing Rock reservation in North Dakota all the way to the headquarters of the US Army Corps of Engineers in Washington, DC, arriving August 6. "We are running for our lives against the Dakota Access Pipeline because it's right in our backyard," said Indigenous activist Bobbi Jean Three Legs. "Now is the time for the people to hear our voices that we are here and we will stand strong." They brought along with them a petition signed by more than 140,000 people from all walks of life. By September of 2016, runner Alice Brown Otter reported that the list had grown to 252,000. "We opened so many hearts and eyes and ears with just our young voices," said Alice that September. They encouraged people to join them on their journey and follow them on social media using #ReZpectOurWater.

The teens' message spread all over the United States, including in Colorado, where Cullen Lobe was studying at Colorado State University. Before he began his activism at Bella Romero, he traveled to Standing Rock Sioux Reservation to make his voice heard in support of the water protectors. He viewed the struggle against fracking and the effort to protect the water of Standing Rock as part of an ongoing war dating to 1492 that

Protest art created in solidarity for the Standing Rock water protectors displayed on a New York City street

has pitted colonists, corporations, and the US government against Indigenous people and others protecting the earth.

On his first night at the reservation in November 2016, Lobe witnessed tear gas, water cannons, rubber bullets, pepper spray, and concussion grenades being used on the nonviolent activists. "I watched as the United States government unleashed a level of violence that still makes me physically sick to this day, all to protect the corporations that own the pipeline," he later recalled.

Lobe wasn't alone in his mission to help the water protectors stop the construction of the Dakota Access Pipeline. Residents of Flint also traveled to Standing Rock to lend their voices and bring supplies. Their ranks included Indigenous (Tlingit/Grand Ronde) activist Trina Redner. She served as a

The Standing Rock camp drew water protectors from all over the world.

supply runner to bring food, water, and other goods to the people remaining and camping on the reservation. She recalled the efforts of Flint neighbors to support the Standing Rock community, saying: "They understood how important water was and how many poisonings of that water supply would affect the entire country," she said.

Kereama Te Ua, a Maori from New Zealand, also joined the cause. On a bitter, cold day in 2016, he stood in the middle of a snowy road leading to Standing Rock and performed the ceremonial *haka*. The stirring, traditional dance displays strength and unity. "It was really about my ancestors acknowledging their ancestors and letting them know that we're here to support them . . . standing for Standing Rock," Kereama Te Ua later said of the dance.

In the fall of 2016, flags from more than three hundred Indigenous nations lined both sides of the road to Standing Rock. Indigenous people had come from all over the world to resist the assault on the reservation from those more concerned with the land's uses than its meaning. For tribal members, the land and the water they protect are sacred, and they had already lost so much land to the US government over the centuries. This was a fight to protect what was left.

"The biggest challenge that faces Indian Country is
that we are all on the front lines. We know what our purpose is.
Our purpose is to protect the earth. So, we're being assaulted
every minute of every day by this society who thinks that
they have a right, their manifest destiny is to control this land
and control all the people and all the animals in it. We can't
give up for a single minute, and we are exhausted."
—Trina Redner, activist

Destruction of a Burial Ground

In addition to the threats to Indian Country's water, the Dakota Access Pipeline brought destruction to the land. In September 2016, pipeline bulldozers plowed through a burial ground that was under review by the US government for historical significance.

ESCALATIONS

Standing Rock became a battlefield.

On the September 2016 anniversary of the Whitestone Hill massacre of September 3, 1863—when the US Army killed more than three hundred members of the Standing Rock Sioux tribe—the water protectors, including women and children, were met with attacks from guard dogs and mace from private security contractors hired by the pipeline oil companies.

As demonstrations continued, Tommy Orange, the Indigenous award-winning author of *There There*, described the scene: The "private militia spent the week of Thanksgiving shooting Native protesters with rubber bullets and spraying us with freezing water . . . And then we saw them trying to get rid of us like time never moved, like the Indian wars didn't end, just went cold."

Reporter and First Nations activist Sarah Sunshine Manning tweeted: "In 1493 Spaniards used war dogs to kill Natives in the name of Gold. Today, Dakota Access uses attack dogs against Natives in the name of oil."

Still, the water protectors persisted, even as the approaching winter brought harsh winds and bitter cold. They had too much to lose to stop their demonstrations. And they weren't alone. There were protests throughout the country in support of Standing Rock.

Amid these protests and various court orders, pipeline construction started and stopped.

Then came the arrests of activists and journalists covering the Standing Rock story. Militarized police confiscated cameras from journalists filming the protests. The Committee to Protect Journalists was aware of at least ten journalists who were facing charges, including Amy Goodman. The award-winning host of the TV show *Democracy Now!* was arrested after filming

Two Sides

Not all the voices raised at Standing Rock were against the pipeline. For many, the pipeline represented energy independence, jobs for Americans, and profits for energy companies. "It all comes down to energy security," said Cory Bryson, business manager for Local 563 of the Laborers International Union. The pipeline would create about three thousand jobs, and Bryson believed it would be completed safely. When pipeline protesters marched through his hometown of Bismarck, North Dakota, Bryson said, "We don't see eye to eye, but at the same time, they have every right to do it."

guard dogs attacking protesters. Jill Stein, a 2016 presidential candidate, was also arrested. All told, more than five hundred people were arrested that fall at Standing Rock, including people against the pipeline, for the pipeline, and those reporting from the site.

HOPES RAISED AND DASHED

After months of debate and protests, the administration of President Barack Obama suspended construction; it also ordered that Energy Transfer Partners prepare an environmental impact statement and study alternate pipeline routes that would not adversely affect the reservation. This was in December 2016, just a month before President Obama would leave the White House. The water protectors were hopeful that their sacred land and water might be protected.

It was a cause for celebration. Cries of relief, singing, and whoops of joy rose from the crowds still encamped at the site. Drumbeats matched the steps in the victory march around the camp, and fireworks lit up the night sky. The protesters had been heard. They had made an impact.

But the celebrations were short-lived. Hope and relief ended the first week of Donald Trump's presidency in January 2017. On his fifth day as president, Trump canceled President Obama's orders. He then approved the final leg of construction. The president said: "The Dakota Access pipeline is now officially open for business. A $3.8-billion investment in American infrastructure was stalled. Nobody thought any politician would have the guts to approve the final leg. And I just closed my eyes and said: 'Do it.'" He added, "It's up, it's running, it's beautiful, it's great. Everybody is happy, the sun is shining, the water's still clean."

But not everyone was happy. When the pipeline became operational in June 2017, it was a devastating blow to thousands of people around the country and the world who supported the Standing Rock water protectors, and who had raised their voices to advocate for clean water, environmental justice, and the rights of Indigenous people.

Between 2012 and 2020, Energy Transfer and its subsidiaries were responsible for 349 leaks, spills, and other accidents. Despite numerous spills and leaks, in 2018 Dakota Access LLC submitted a new proposal to double the flow of oil through the pipeline from 570,000 to 1.1 million barrels (77,760 to 150,068 metric tonnes) per day, which would increase the risk to the water on the reservation. Earthjustice attorney Jan Hasselman represented the tribe. He remarked in response to the new proposal: "This is a company under criminal investigation for negligence—it should not be allowed to operate a food truck, let alone a major crude oil pipeline."

A LIGHT AT THE END OF THE TUNNEL

In February 2019, it was reported that an Army Corps of Engineers document proved that the agency had disregarded a federal judge's order to review the potential impact of the pipeline on the Standing Rock Sioux and other Dakota tribes.

In response to the July 6, 2020, order by the US District Court for the District of Columbia to shut down DAPL by August 5, 2020, Standing Rock Sioux tribal chairman Mike Faith said in a statement: "This pipeline should have never been built here. We told them that from the beginning."

On January 19, 2021, just one day before President Joe Biden took office, the leaders of tribes including the Standing Rock Sioux, Cheyenne River Sioux, Oglala Sioux, and Yankton

Sioux sent a letter to the president-elect requesting quick action to honor the treaties made with the United States and to "respect our lands and our waters, and stop this illegal pipeline."

Although President Biden took quick action to issue an executive order on his first day in office to cancel the equally troubling Keystone XL pipeline, he did not act in those first days of his presidency to put an end to the Dakota Access Pipeline. Pressure for him to do so mounted. ◊

Pipelines Leak

The Dakota Access Pipeline was not the only pipeline project green-lighted by the Trump administration. TransCanada Corp's Keystone pipeline and the Belle Fourche pipeline were both greenlighted by his administration, and both leaked hundreds of thousands of gallons of crude oil in the Dakotas.

In 2017, the Keystone pipeline had a major leak of an estimated 407 thousand gallons (more than 1.5 million liters) onto South Dakota farmland (and this wasn't the first spill—there had been another in 2011). Then, in 2019, the pipeline leaked roughly 383,000 gallons (1.4 million liters) of oil in North Dakota, affecting .52 acres (.21 hectares) of land in Edinburg, near the Canadian border.

The Belle Fourche pipeline spilled 529,830 gallons (more than 2 million liters) of oil in March 2017, contaminating a hillside and Ash Coulee Creek outside Belfield, North Dakota. Cleanup crews found traces of carcinogenic benzene at the site. To recover the oil in the creek, contractors performed twelve hundred controlled burns on the floating layer of oil. Although the spill didn't affect any human drinking water sources, the rancher suffered a loss of cattle at the site.

FRACKING—THE GLOBAL THREAT

The Dakota Access Pipeline story drew global attention, but there are so many other stories like this around the world. Pipelines for oil and gas are weaving a web around our planet. With them come accidents. Millions of gallons of oil have spilled from pipelines in Canada, India, Mexico, Nigeria, Russia, and Taiwan.

All these incidents became environmental disasters—the oil spills polluted drinking water and wetland habitats and damaged communities around the world.

All energy derived from fossil fuels, from coal burning to oil drilling and transport, comes with a cost that is inextricably tied to water. All these costs can be reduced when we conserve energy. Conservation and regulations hold the industry accountable and keep us healthy. Green alternatives, like solar power, eliminate some of the risks tied to fossil fuels. These things should be on our minds when we turn on our lights, as we listen to the news, and as we vote.

FROM ENERGY TO AGRICULTURE

As detailed previously, most fossil fuel energy manufacturing takes place in rural areas. But energy isn't the only major industry adversely affecting the water in these regions. There's also agriculture. Growing, producing, and processing our food also comes with risks and costs to our water supply. The pollution isn't always as visible as other industrial pollution, but it can be just as damaging. ◊

CHAPTER 4: FARM TO WATER— AGRICULTURAL POLLUTION

THE SCENE IS BUCOLIC—miles of green pasture dotted by barns and cows. What could be more tranquil? But despite its serenity, beautiful farmland in America and other parts of the world isn't immune to facing—or contributing to—water contamination. Farms, especially large commercial farms, often manage their land with chemical pesticides, weed-killing herbicides, and fertilizers that can contaminate ecosystems and our drinking water.

Between 1950 and 1980, synthetic organic pesticide production tripled in the United States from 400 million pounds (181 million kilograms) to 1.4 billion pounds (635 million kilograms). Today, we still use over 1 billion pounds (453 million kilograms) of pesticides each year in the United States and over 5 billion pounds (2.27 billion kilograms) worldwide. These chemicals, which are designed to kill crop-eating pests and increase the amount of food we grow, have consequences. Sometimes, those consequences are too great, and a pesticide must be banned from use, as was the case with DDT. This pesticide was designed to kill insects that damaged crops, but it almost took the US population of bald eagles and other species with it as it made its way through the ecosystem food chains before being banned in 1972.

Once a pesticide has been determined to be dangerous, the pathway to banning its use can take many twists and turns. This was the case for a pesticide called aldicarb that polluted Long Island's water over thirty years ago. It was still being used in the fields of Georgia and Florida until a federal appeals court rejected its use in June of 2021.

CASE STUDY: LONG ISLAND, FLORIDA, AND BEYOND— THE PATH OF PESTICIDE POLLUTION

Finding Long Island, New York, on a map is easy. The island juts out from New York City's shoreline into the Atlantic Ocean, stretching northeast along the state of Connecticut. Like many islands, it has sandy soil. It also has a shallow water table, meaning its groundwater is close to the surface of the earth. Unlike in the five boroughs of New York City, which pipe in water from upstate, all the residents of Long Island—whether they live in the upscale Hamptons or the more densely residential and manufacturing areas—draw their drinking water from the shallow water table. Adding a mix of manufacturing and agricultural waste to Long Island's sandy soil and shallow water table can be a perfect recipe for pollution problems. Whatever is on the soil surface can easily end up in the water below.

That's exactly what happened over fifty years ago, when a pesticide called aldicarb—sold under the brand name Temik—was used for four growing seasons on more than 2,000 acres (809 hectares) of Long Island farmland. The pesticide was manufactured by Union Carbide Corporation, a subsidiary of Dow Chemical, and was used initially to control two Long Island agricultural pests—the Colorado potato beetle and the golden nematode. According to the EPA, aldicarb is "highly toxic to humans and wildlife." It affects the nervous system and can lead to many long-term health issues, including cancer and birth defects.

The pesticide was first detected in Long Island's Suffolk County groundwater in August 1979. A monitoring program conducted by Suffolk County in cooperation with federal and state agencies revealed that 1,121 wells out of 8,404 exceeded the federal limit of 7 ppb. About half of those contaminated wells contained between 8 ppb and 30 ppb of aldicarb, while 32 percent were even higher, falling between 31 and 75 ppb. Some even exceeded 75 ppb.

Charcoal filters were distributed to thousands of residents who had contaminated water, and in June 1980, Union Carbide voluntarily asked the EPA to ban the pesticide.

But the EPA didn't ban the pesticide. Instead, in 1981, it classified the pesticide as a restricted use compound in the United States, meaning users had to be cleared before using it. This reclassification didn't prohibit the use of aldicarb or prevent contaminations. Although everyone permitted to use aldicarb had to be trained and certified, the pesticide still found its way into misuse and was still being manufactured abroad.

Its Bhopal, India, pesticide plant became the site of the worst industrial chemical accident on the planet when, on December 3, 1984, a toxic cloud of methyl isocyanate and other gases used in pesticide production was released into the air. The toxic cloud exposed over five hundred thousand people, killing almost four thousand that night, causing the deaths of as many as twenty thousand more, and injuring tens of thousands. The area and its water remain toxic to this day.

TEMIK® brand 10G ALDICARB PESTICIDE

For Control of Certain Insects, Mites, and Nematodes

ACTIVE INGREDIENT: Aldicarb [2-methyl-2-(methylthio) propionaldehydeO-(methylcarbamoyl)oxime] 10%
INERT INGREDIENTS: 90%

EPA Reg. No. 264-331   EPA Est. No. 10352-GA-01

KEEP OUT OF REACH OF CHILDREN
DANGER   POISON
PELIGRO

PRECAUCION AL USARIO: Si usted no lee ingles, no use este producto hasta que le etiqueta haya sido explicado ampliamente.
TRANSLATION TO THE USER: If you cannot read English, do not use this product until the label has been fully explained to you.)

For **MEDICAL** And **TRANSPORTATION** Emergencies **ONLY** Call 24 Hours A Day 1-800-334-7577
For **PRODUCT USE** Information Call 1-800-334-9745

STATEMENT OF PRACTICAL TREATMENT

IF SWALLOWED: Drink 1 or 2 glasses of water and induce vomiting by touching back of throat with finger. Do not induce vomiting or give anything orally to an unconscious or convulsing person. Call a physician and follow General advice listed below.

IF IN EYES: Flush eyes with plenty of water and get medical attention.

IF ON SKIN: Wash thoroughly with soap and water. Remove contaminated clothing and wash before reuse.

IF INHALED: Call a physician and follow General advice listed below.

Pesticides like Temik (aldicarb) can have immediate yet long-lasting effects on human health.

And the contaminations in the US weren't affecting just Long Island: Levels of the pesticide showed up in watermelons in California on July 4, 1985, and over a thousand people became ill. Thirteen years later, in July 1998, a company picnic in Louisiana turned into a disaster when aldicarb was improperly stored, mistaken for black pepper, and used in food preparation. Ten picnickers sought help at an emergency room, and two were hospitalized. Anyone who had ingested a small six-gram portion of the cabbage salad at the picnic had inadvertently consumed 272.6 ppm of aldicarb. Although this incident didn't contaminate any water, it proved that the pesticide's restricted use classification didn't make it safe.

In 2010, the pesticide was still showing up in Long Island wells, over thirty years after the initial contamination. That same year, Bayer CropScience, which had begun producing Temik (aldicarb), voluntarily announced that it would phase out production of the pesticide in cooperation with the EPA, which (based on risk assessments) had decreased the amounts that would be allowed in food. The plan came in the wake of studies that proved high levels of the pesticide led to many health concerns, including blurred vision and nausea. Bayer CropScience indicated that Temik use for potatoes and citrus would cease at the end of 2011, and its worldwide use in all ways would end by 2014. Still, the EPA did not ban its use.

In 2016, the new chemical corporation AgLogic set out to return the pesticide to agricultural use. "It's become obvious over the past five years that the loss of TEMIK has created significant pest control challenges for many growers across a wide range of crops," the corporation's CEO and president, Dr. Antoine A. Puech, stated in a press release.

The pesticide was renamed AgLogic 15G and went back into use in 2016, again under a restricted use EPA policy requiring certification. In 2020, the pesticide was registered in almost half of America's states, including Virginia, North Carolina, South Carolina, Georgia, Florida, Texas, Michigan, Colorado, Kansas, Idaho, Washington, and Oregon. In January 2021, the EPA approved the use of aldicarb to be used on up to 100,000 acres (40,470 hectares) in Florida groves of oranges and grapefruits to combat greening disease, which has harmed Florida's citrus industry. Specific restrictions were put in place to protect potential runoff and drinking water sources. Although banned in over one hundred countries, the pesticide can still be found in some, including Brazil.

The administration of Brazil's president, Jair Bolsonaro, has a robust agribusiness lobby that has pushed for the deregulation of pesticides and other agriculture compounds. Many of these toxic pesticides and herbicides, including AgLogic 15G, are produced by American corporations. Even though many are banned or have restricted use in the United States, they are often still used abroad; some are even smuggled in for use.

In Brazil, aldicarb has been detected in 10 out of 26 stomach samples of endangered tapirs. One 2019 report of samples collected from 116 tapirs indicated that 40 percent of them were contaminated with pesticides and other chemicals. ◀

IT ISN'T JUST ALDICARB

The story of aldicarb shows how harmful pesticides can come back into use in the United States even after being phased out. Sometimes, this back-and-forth movement is the result of a turnover in federal administrations.

For example, EPA scientists recommended placing a ban on the pesticide chlorpyrifos in 2017 because it was found to be harmful to children and farmworkers. The EPA, however, decided against the ban after Donald Trump took office in January 2017 and changed the leadership of that agency. By 2020, there was still controversy swirling as cases of pollution and poisonings from chlorpyrifos continued to occur.

This story is repeated in the reapproval of the chemical glyphosate, which is commonly known as an active ingredient in Monsanto Company's Roundup herbicides. After it was found to cause cancer, threatened countless wildlife species, and was deemed unsafe by the World Health Organization in 2016, it was reapproved by the EPA in January 2020. A coalition of farmworkers, farmers, and conservationists have joined together to file a federal lawsuit against the EPA for the reapproval of this toxic pesticide that can damage our water and our wildlife.

As the world's population grows, requiring the production of more food, it becomes ever more essential to strive for sustainable agricultural practices that require less chemical interaction, enhance our food security, and keep our water clean.

FERTILIZERS

Not all agricultural pollution issues stem from pesticides and herbicides. The nitrate- and phosphorous-rich fertilizers used by the farming industry to enrich soil can also lead to water contamination.

Nitrate is an essential, life-giving nutrient for plants. It helps them make proteins and is important for healthy plant growth, which is why it is often used as a nitrogen compound in fertilizers. Nitrates can be added to soil by spreading animal manure or coffee grounds, planting nitrogen-rich crops like peas and beans, or through the use of chemical fertilizers. Whatever the source of the nitrates, these substances can find their way into our drinking water. And while nitrates are essential for plants, they are dangerous for humans.

INTO THE GROUNDWATER

It's easy to see how groundwater can become contaminated. Picture a cross-section of the earth's layers. The first layer is the topsoil. The second is the sand. The third is rock. Finally, there's water. When a farmer adds nitrates to the topsoil, it seeps or percolates down through the layers into the groundwater below.

Manure in particular has become a significant cause of water contamination around the world. Farm crews are supposed to spread only the amount of manure their crops can use; often, however, so much is applied that it surpasses the ground's natural absorption rate. All that manure releases nitrates that seep through the soil into the groundwater below or run off into other water sources.

Why are nitrates such a problem? High levels of nitrates in water affect our red blood cells' ability to carry oxygen. Long-term exposure to nitrates during childhood has resulted in stunted growth in adulthood. Elevated nitrate levels can cause methemoglobinemia, or "blue baby" disease, a condition that damages a baby's heart, and it's also suspected of causing cancer, thyroid issues, and congenital disabilities.

In 2017, the Food and Agriculture Organization of the United Nations reported that nitrates from agriculture are the most common pollutant in the world's groundwater. It's a global problem that is especially prevalent in America's heartland, where nitrate contamination threatens the quality of the wells near dairy farms where manure is stored and used. In recent years, we've seen this play out in Wisconsin.

CASE STUDY: KEWAUNEE COUNTY, WISCONSIN— CONTAMINATION IN COW COUNTRY

Retired Wisconsin truck driver Arlin Karnopp stopped drinking the water at his home in Kewaunee County, where cows outnumber people by a five-to-one ratio. He placed a sign on his refrigerator that read "Do Not Use" to remind his grandchildren not to use the ice from the dispenser on the door.

He blamed the high nitrate and bacteria levels in his well water on the manure used as fertilizer by a nearby dairy farm.

"Everything rolls downhill," Arlin said in a 2019 interview with the *Milwaukee Journal Sentinel*.

The average cow releases about a pound (454 grams) of nitrogen a day in its urine and feces.

DAIRY FARM POLLUTION

The state of Wisconsin boasts more than ninety-five hundred dairy farms with over a million cows. Not long ago, most of the state's dairy farms were small, family operations, but many have gone out of business as large industrial farms have replaced them. Wisconsin isn't alone in losing dairy farms. The US dairy herd shrank by a million animals between 2018 and 2019, with roughly 2,500 dairies going out of business in 2018. The megafarm operations are known as concentrated animal feeding operations. Rather than having an average of 150 cows, these factory farms often have 700 or more.

A lot of cows means a lot of cow manure, so it's no surprise that Wisconsin residents have found their wells contaminated by high levels of nitrates. The wells can be contaminated by sewage overflows, improperly working sewage systems, polluted stormwater, and agricultural runoff.

About 97 percent of Wisconsin communities rely on groundwater from more than eight hundred thousand private wells. A 2019 study led by Mark Borchardt, a research microbiologist for the US Agricultural Research Service, tested thirty-five wells and found that thirty-two of them were contaminated from fecal matter from humans or livestock. The testing showed that contamination from seventeen of the wells came from cattle, and pigs caused contamination in five wells. During 2016–2017, a test by Borchardt in another part of the state also found widespread cattle contamination, with levels that far exceeded the state and federal standards. Wisconsin follows the EPA MCL in water for nitrates set at 10 ppm and for nitrites 1 ppm.

"As a researcher of groundwater for 25 years now, I continue to be amazed by the level of fecal contamination in Wisconsin groundwater," said Borchardt in an August 2019 Associated Press article. 💧

"This is not how we should be living. We've lost the value in the house and everyone says it's not their fault. I want it to stop."
—Mary Lou Karnopp, Arlin Karnopp's wife

Rotavirus

The wells Mark Borchardt tested in Wisconsin didn't contain only nitrates. Many of them also contained illness-causing pathogens such as salmonella and rotavirus, which pose global threats. Severe diarrhea is a leading cause of death worldwide. Children younger than five years old are at an even greater risk. Rotavirus, which can cause severe diarrhea, is responsible for 215,000 deaths annually worldwide. Most occurred in South Asia and sub-Saharan Africa.

OPEN-WATER CONTAMINATION

Not all the compounds in manure seep into groundwater. Some of them wash into open water, where they can cause an overgrowth of algae, a process called eutrophication. Next, let's investigate how algal blooms—including red tides—affect open water and pose threats to marine ecosystems and humans. 💧

CHAPTER 5: WHEN THE WATER RUNS RED— HARMFUL ALGAL BLOOMS (HABS) AND RED TIDES

TWO MILES (3.2 kilometers) within the forests of northwestern Michigan's Isle Royale National Park, one of the most remote—and the least visited—of America's national parks, is small Lake Richie with a nasty odor. Why would a lake on an island in the middle of a Great Lake stink? The smell is the result of a serious outbreak of a toxic blue-green algae.

Algal outbreaks like this have occurred in urban, suburban, and rural areas where runoff of phosphorus- and nitrogen-rich fertilizer from fields and lawns reaches waterways. Although some algal blooms aren't harmful, many produce cyanotoxins that harm fish, other animals, and people. The excess phosphorous and nitrogen can spur the growth of a cyanobacteria, which consume the oxygen in the water and block life-giving sunlight from reaching underwater plants. These harmful algal blooms, or HABs, have shut down beaches and, more importantly, poisoned water supplies. Touching the blue-green algae layer on the water's surface can lead to skin, eye, and ear irritations, and if swallowed, the algae can cause stomach cramps, sore throat, diarrhea, fever, headaches, muscle and joint pain, and even liver and nerve damage.

While most of these outbreaks can be explained by nutrient-rich runoff, scientists are perplexed by how a small lake in the middle of Isle Royale National Park's pristine wilderness—far from any farms—can be so adversely affected.

Isle Royale National Park ecologist Lynette Potvin routinely hikes to secluded Wallace Lake to monitor the water. Her time-sensitive samples are delivered by the National Park Service ferry across Lake Superior to a scientist waiting in Houghton, Michigan, to run to the laboratory for testing.

"We've had some cyanobacteria outbreaks, harmful algal blooms, but they are rare for a system like this because we don't have farm fields draining into our lakes," she said in 2019.

Researchers explored the possibility that the large local moose population had stirred up lake-bottom muck on Isle Royale, releasing nutrients into the warm water and contributing to the high phosphorous levels in the lake. But a later study ruled out that possibility.

It is puzzling to find algal bloom outbreaks in remote areas like Isle Royale National Park.

Could these nutrients have flown across the country on the wind and landed in Lake Richie? That's very possible. Lakes like this one, far from any pollution source, might be victims of dustfall, which originates miles away and is borne into the atmosphere. In 2020, the Science Museum of Minnesota's St. Croix Watershed Research Station was planning to work with the Minnesota Pollution Control Agency and the National Park Service to monitor sixteen lakes across the region to measure the dustfall.

Whatever the source, algal bloom outbreaks like the ones affecting Lake Wallace and Lake Richie are becoming more prevalent as the earth warms due to climate change. Decreasing ice coverage on many lakes means that there is, on average, an extra month of open water for sunlight to fuel algae and cyanobacteria growth.

And cyanobacteria outbreaks, which occur in all fifty American states, aren't limited to small lakes and ponds. The cyanobacteria outbreak in nearby Lake Erie, another of America's five Great Lakes, is proof.

CASE STUDY: LAKE ERIE—HARMFUL ALGAL BLOOMS

For many residents of Toledo, Ohio, there's nothing more enjoyable than a cool dip in a lake on a hot summer day. But during the summer of 2014, residents visiting the nearby public beach on Lake Erie found Danger signs warning them to avoid all contact with the water. A cyanobacteria outbreak was to blame. And it didn't just affect swimming access—because Lake Erie is a source of drinking water for twelve million people in the United States and Canada, it cut off 500 thousand Toledo residents from their drinking water for three days and caused 110 people to become ill.

Although the bacteria that was contaminating the lake

does occur naturally, the conditions that caused the outbreak that summer were human-made.

Scientists have been measuring the pollution in the rivers and streams flowing into Lake Erie for decades. They've found that the agricultural industry and sewage in the region have caused phosphorous to flow into the waters, fueling the growth of cyanobacteria in the lake's warm, shallow regions.

Industrial contamination also plays a role. The Lake Erie Basin includes five US states and the province of Ontario, Canada. Within that area are more than 10 thousand square miles (25,900 square kilometers) of farmland as well as the urban centers of Fort Wayne, Indiana; Detroit, Michigan; Toledo and Cleveland, Ohio; Erie, Pennsylvania; and Buffalo, New York. All these areas, full of industrial and agricultural industry, could be potential polluters.

POINT AND NONPOINT SOURCE POLLUTION

The pollution in Lake Erie is classified in two ways. The first is point source pollution, which includes the contamination coming straight into the lake through pipes from factories and water treatment plants.

The second is nonpoint source pollution. This includes agricultural runoff into the streams that feed the lake. Although the primary inflow of water into Lake Erie is from the Detroit River, water also flows into the lake from the upper Great Lakes—Superior, Michigan, and Huron—and from a number of tributaries. All those rivers have the potential of raising the levels of pollution in the lake. In fact, the runoff coming from those rivers into the lake accounts for 72 percent of the lake's phosphorous.

That's why agricultural management is crucial to protect the lake and keep the water safe to drink. Everyone has to play a part in preserving the lake's water quality, especially as the situation becomes more dire—since 2014, the growing threat of algal blooms has only increased, with 2015 and 2019 being record years for Lake Erie. The blue-green water in 2019 was even visible from space.

So what action has been taken to fix Lake Erie's water problems?

REGULATION AND ACTION

The Federal Water Pollution Control Act of 1948 was amended by the US Congress in 1972 as the Clean Water Act. The new act was designed to protect the American public from water pollution, and it also gave the EPA authority to implement pollution control and the ability to set standards. While it strengthened the protections, like many regulations, it also contained loopholes that enabled special interests—including agriculture—to get around the monitoring process. When federal regulations fail to do their job, sometimes states have to step in, as Ohio did in the case of Lake Erie.

Ohio passed a law after the 2014 crisis prohibiting farmers in the region from spreading phosphorous-rich fertilizer on rain-soaked or frozen soil, which could lead to further runoff into waterways. Another law went into effect in 2017 requiring farmers to take a certification course to learn more about fertilizer application. These were important steps, but they didn't go far enough. A bigger step forward would have been to legally mandate farmers to use only the minimal amount of fertilizer for their crops. Currently, the majority of efforts to control runoff are voluntary—and unfortunately, when efforts are voluntary, they are often not taken seriously.

There has been some progress, however. In 2016, The EPA developed the US Action Plan for Lake Erie under the Great Lakes Water Quality Agreement to reduce phosphorus pollution. This commitment and strategy was targeted to take place from 2018 to 2023. Monitoring was put in place, and every three to five years the EPA planned to analyze the progress. 💧

Mayfly Deaths

Mayflies are a vital keystone species in the freshwater ecosystems where nymphs mature into adults. Many other species in these ecosystems, including dragonflies, crayfish, and many fish species, depend on them for food. The mayfly population in Lake Erie has plummeted due to the increase in pesticide use, algal blooms, and the higher water temperatures brought on by climate change. Because these insects do well only in clean water, they are an important indicator species for water quality.

Steps You Can Take to Curb Algal Blooms and Keep Healthy

1. Rinse off after lake swims.

2. Use phosphate-free soaps, laundry detergent, and lawn products.

3. Wash cars on the lawn to avoid runoff.

4. Pick up after your pet.

5. Do not dump household chemicals into street gutters or storm drains.

Tracking HABs

You can follow Lake Erie's HAB forecast daily at the NOAA Tides and Currents: Lake Erie Harmful Algal Bloom Forecast website. Explore worldwide HABs through the UNESCO Intergovernmental Oceanographic Commission website.

INTO THE SEA

Nonpoint pollution affects not only the water quality of Lake Erie and other inland lakes. According to the National Oceanic and Atmospheric Administration (NOAA), it's also believed to be the greatest threat to US coastal waters. It contributes to coral reef bleaching and dead zones, areas along the coasts where nothing can live.

One of the most widely known HABs involves the poisoning of marine life and forcing the closure of beaches along the shoreline of the Gulf of Mexico. Instead of an outbreak of cyanobacteria that appears as blue-green algae, this HAB is caused by dinoflagellates, single-celled algae occurring in marine plankton that turn the water a muddy red. That's why HABs like this one are called red tides.

The smell of a red tide is often the first sign of its presence. Winds carry airborne red tide particles to coastal areas where residents notice their noses tingle and burn. The second sign is the carcasses of marine life that cover the beaches. Like a cyanobacteria outbreak, red tides produce harmful neurotoxins that cause the death of fish, sea turtles, birds, and marine mammals. They can also cause widespread respiratory problems in humans. In addition, these neurotoxins can accumulate in shellfish, causing neurotoxic shellfish poisoning. People, in turn, can consume these shellfish at beachside restaurants.

Like blue-green algae outbreaks, red tides are caused by the runoff of sediments, agricultural pesticides, and fertilizers, but other factors contribute to red tide events, including warming ocean temperatures and low salinity levels. Red tides are more frequent when rainy days that facilitate runoff are followed by sunny days that contribute to bacteria growth in the water.

Florida has been especially hard hit by red tides over the years. In 2013, a red tide of *Karenia brevis* algae killed almost three hundred manatees, and from 2017 to 2019, a mixture of rain, runoff, and sunshine created a perfect storm that gave rise to red tides in the southwestern part of the state.

Coral Reef Pollution

Coral reefs are hubs of biodiversity and play a critical role in ocean ecosystems. They also help protect shorelines from wave and storm damage. But they are fragile. Agricultural runoff can coat coral and kill it. Other threats include sediment runoff from deforestation, coastal development, road construction, and failed septic systems. Oil and chemical spills also contribute to the death of coral reefs.

CASE STUDY: SOUTHWEST FLORIDA—RED TIDES

Florida's 2017–2019 HAB event claimed millions of pounds of fish and other marine life. It emptied beaches, resorts, and beachside restaurants in the summer of 2018. It was the longest outbreak in over a decade and impacted over 100 miles (160 kilometers) of Florida coastline.

The popular barrier island of Sanibel Island, Florida, was hit especially hard. The body of a twenty-six-foot whale shark washed up on a Sanibel beach in July 2018, filled with the algal toxin. But that wasn't all. Dr. Heather Barron, the veterinarian who runs the Clinic for the Rehabilitation of Wildlife on Sanibel

Island, saw four times the number of sea turtles poisoned during this time. The wildlife death toll was astronomical, from endangered manatees to dolphins and pelicans. "We have had as many as one hundred patients come in, in two days, all affected with red tide," Dr. Barron said in an interview with PBS.

It wasn't just wildlife that suffered—beachgoers, tourists, outdoor diners, and coastal businesses were also impaired by the contaminated waters. Lifeguards in Sarasota had to don gas masks to stay safe.

Governor Rick Scott, who was largely criticized for cutting roughly $700 million from the state's environmental agencies that oversee algae outbreaks, declared a state of emergency on August 13, 2018. His opponents nicknamed him Red Tide Rick.

Why was the bloom so much worse during these years? Timing and a changing climate. In September 2017, Hurricane Irma made landfall and soaked Florida with rain. In November that year, the US Army Corps of Engineers attempted to prevent flooding by releasing water from Lake Okeechobee. The lake's waters, loaded with fertilizer, flowed into the warm ocean. It is believed that the nutrient-rich runoff, warm water, decreased salinity, sunlight, and the Gulf of Mexico currents all combined to create a recipe for disaster.

Ecologists who explored the waters during these years found that the concentration of red tide–causing *Karenia brevis* algae was roughly ten times higher than for an average event, according to Richard Bartleson, a marine biologist at Sanibel-Captiva Conservation Foundation. During a usual red tide event, between one hundred thousand and two hundred thousand cells are generally found in a liter of seawater, but during this event, ecologists found two million to twenty million cells in a liter.

Hundreds of Florida residents gathered for the Hands Along the Water event along the coastlines of the state on August 12, 2018, to bring awareness and much-needed action to mitigate red tide events.

Although this red tide event ended after two years in 2019, the Florida Fish and Wildlife Conservation Commission has continued to sample and monitor the waters for similar events.

In addition, residents and conservationists have continued to focus on efforts to control and regulate nutrients entering Florida waterways. ◖

RED TIDES ON GLOBAL SHORES

Red tides occur all over the world, from the United States to the Philippines, from Australia to Japan. For example, in August 2017, just as the disastrous red tide was about to hit Florida, fish farmers in Japan suffered from the loss of about 270,000 puffer fish from a toxic HAB red tide. Puffers, although lethally poisonous if not handled properly, are one of the country's most celebrated and luxurious delicacies. The disaster led to the loss of about $400 million Japanese yen ($3.8 million US at the time).

While red tides have been recorded for centuries—including several reports mentioned in the three-hundred-year-old history book *Dai-nihon-shi* (*The History of Great Japan*)—they are becoming more prevalent and more damaging due to warming temperatures and increased agricultural and sewage runoff.

ANOTHER SOURCE OF POLLUTION

There's plentiful evidence that everything we spread across the land, including fertilizers, herbicides, and pesticides, can negatively affect

the quality of our water, posing threats to humans, wildlife, and the environment. But there's another source of pollution contaminating our water that is important to address: *accidental pollution*, which refers to human medication entering waterways. In the next chapter, we'll take a closer look at the threats accidental pollution poses and what we can do about it. 💧

Protecting stormwater from contamination in Fort Collins, Colorado.

CHAPTER 6: DRUGS IN THE WATER— PHARMACEUTICALS AND ACCIDENTAL POLLUTION

DR. ERINN RICHMOND, an ecologist at Monash University in Melbourne, Australia, waded into six creeks around Melbourne in 2014 and 2015. Her research team scooped up insect larvae, snails, and other creek critters. Tests showed something surprising—seventy different human medications found within the bodies of the creatures collected.

This study to find out more about accidental pollution—the pollution that happens when medicines designed for human needs find their way into waterways—was alarming because there were so many affected creatures, and most of them were part of the diet of other animals, including iconic Australian platypuses. Each creature that ingests contaminated smaller organisms also ingests the pharmaceutical poisons they've consumed. Each level up the food chain increases the medication levels in the animals digesting them.

A platypus living at the most contaminated creek likely ingested about half a human dosage of antidepressants every day, plus any other medications in the water. This concerned researchers, who wondered how it would affect the animal's long-term health.

"If you or I went to the doctor and said we're taking 69 different drugs, they'd probably have a heart attack," said Dr. Richmond in an article about her published paper in *Nature Communications*.

Pharmaceuticals in waterways is a growing global problem. "Last year, pharmaceuticals were found in surface water in Antarctica," Dr. Richmond explained. "It's getting increasingly harder to find pristine, uncontaminated sites."

But where do these medications come from, and how do they enter the water?

THE PATH OF PHARMACEUTICALS

We've seen how animal waste can find its way into fresh water in agricultural areas. It seeps into groundwater from sewage systems and polluted stormwater. Sometimes, that agricultural waste contains antibiotics and other drugs used in the livestock industry to keep animals healthy and increase growth. Streams receiving runoff from animal feeding operations, like the megafarms in Wisconsin, can contain many medicines, including acetaminophen, caffeine, and diphenhydramine.

There are additional ways that medications enter waterways. They can enter in wastewater discharge from pharmaceutical manufacturing plants. This release is monitored in accord with state and federal regulations. But there are other ways as well. In the last days of the Trump administration in January 2021, at the same time the EPA approved the use of aldicarb for use in citrus groves, the federal agency also approved the use of streptomycin, an antibiotic used to treat tuberculosis, to be sprayed on the same citrus crops. About 14,000 pounds (6,350 kilograms) of this strategic antibiotic is used by Americans each year. Being used for citrus could increase that number to hundreds of thousands of pounds being used, and potentially threaten any nearby water supply.

And then there are humans. Our bodies don't absorb all the medications and vitamins we take. The parts of a substance that do not get used by the body are excreted in our waste. Every time we flush a toilet, some of these substances go down the drain. If you have municipal water, the waste goes to the water treatment facility, but not many treatment facilities are equipped to remove all the chemicals that end up in our wastewater. Plus, some of the compounds stick to solid waste that is sometimes spread as sludge on fields. The pharmaceuticals can then seep into the groundwater.

Even in cases where waste is not funneled into a treatment facility—for instance, for septic systems or wells—it can still release drugs into the groundwater system as it passes through layers of filtered soil. From there, the drugs can make their way into streams and rivers, where they enter food webs and affect the health and welfare of wildlife and humans.

Pharmaceuticals also end up in the environment when we flush unused portions away instead of properly disposing of them.

Whatever chemical compounds go down our drains, they have to come out somewhere—and many don't disappear. As a result, there are more than four thousand different prescription medications for humans and animals that end up in our environment. And all of them can affect the health and behavior of insects, birds, fish, and mammals—including humans.

The federal government does not regularly test for these contaminations, but they do maintain a database of pharmaceuticals and personal care products. There are more than fifteen hundred FDA-approved substances that humans and pets use on and in their bodies. All of them can end up in our water.

These substances are already having an impact on wildlife in places like the Chesapeake Bay, an estuary in the mid-Atlantic region bordered by the states of Virginia and Maryland.

It's Not Just Medications

A 2007 report by twenty-nine scientists of the United Kingdom's Royal Society of Chemistry warned about a variety of chemicals from our soaps, body washes, and detergents finding their way from our showers and washing machines into the environment. One of these is the antibacterial chemical triclosan, which has been reported in the bodies of fish and in human breast milk. As detailed for medications, synthetic compounds in these products don't break down in water as easily as natural substances. Check the ingredients in your soaps to see if they are safe for the environment. You may want to make a change to a product that's more environmentally friendly, like castile soap, a vegetable oil–based product that can be used as a body wash and a shampoo.

Tracking Viruses via Wastewater

At the time of writing in 2021, the world is experiencing the COVID-19 pandemic. In an attempt to track the epidemic's movement throughout the world, researchers examined wastewater in several cities in Italy. They found evidence of the virus in samples taken in Milan and Turin in December 2019 and Bologna in January 2020. This showed that the coronavirus was spreading through Italy before the outbreak was fully recognized in the early spring of 2020.

CASE STUDY: THE CHESAPEAKE BAY— SYNTHETIC MEDICATIONS LEAD TO FEMINIZED FISH

Many synthetic medications pose a more significant problem because they are less biodegradable than natural chemicals. That means they don't break down as easily. They can remain in the water system without degrading for an indeterminate time, allowing for more interactions with wildlife.

For example, fish have been "feminized" by ingesting synthetic estrogen from contraceptive pills that have ended up in waterways.

A 2016 survey of fish in nineteen national wildlife refuges in the northeastern US found 60 to 100 percent of all male smallmouth bass had female egg cells growing inside male reproductive organs. Federal scientists first discovered this condition by accident while studying a smallmouth-bass die-off in the Chesapeake Bay in 2003. They found the condition, known as intersex, in more than three-quarters of the fish they studied.

Some species do naturally have both male and female sex organs. They are known as hermaphrodites, and their unique natural adaptation enables them to have successful reproduction. Intersex isn't a natural condition, however, and it doesn't help reproduction. In fact, it can make fish sterile, unable to reproduce and continue the species. If this condition becomes more prevalent, fish populations will suffer, as will the populations of any creature feeding on those fish. Everything is connected. ⬧

ACCIDENTAL POLLUTION: THE BIG PICTURE

Many of us need all sorts of medications for our health and well-being. The growth in our population—specifically among those who are aging and tend to rely on more pharmaceuticals—has caused an increase in the amount of drugs found in the environment and our water supply. In a 2008 survey, the Associated Press found pharmaceutical contamination in twenty-four major US cities. Philadelphia's water contained fifty-six medications, including drugs for pain, infections, asthma, epilepsy, and heart disease, while Southern California's water contained antianxiety drugs and other medications. Just think: When you drink water, you could be ingesting traces of someone else's medications.

There are currently not enough monitoring programs or comprehensive studies on human exposure to pharmaceuticals from drinking water. More studies and tests are needed. Although it is unlikely that exposure to low levels of pharmaceuticals in drinking water significantly affects people's health, according to the World Health Organization, we can't relax our concern. As our population continues to grow and baby boomers age, the rising use of medications will increase the chance that accidental contamination becomes more of a problem. And we aren't prepared in terms of infrastructure to help address this problem. Many treatment plants do not currently have the purifying technology to remove pharmaceutical contamination, and plant updates come with a cost. In addition to being very expensive, updates can create an energy footprint that further harms the environment.

So what can we do? As a start, we can avoid flushing unused drugs down the toilet and instead dispose of them properly. How? Ask at your local pharmacy for disposal information. The staff can point you to a safe location to deposit your unused medications. Some states, including Iowa, Nebraska, and New Hampshire, offer drug take-back programs. If your state or local pharmacist can't help you, put your excess medications into a plastic bag, dissolve them with water, add kitty litter, coffee grounds, or sawdust, and place the bag in the trash. And raise your voice—ask your town officials to host a Drug Take-Back Day for your community.

FROM WATER QUALITY TO WATER QUANTITY

We've explored many different ways that the quality of our water can be impacted, but that's only half the story of our planet's water crisis. The other half has to do with water quantity. What happens when there is too little—or too much—water? Both of these situations can lead to water stress and a host of other issues. 💧

CHAPTER 7: DRY WELLS AND DAY ZERO— WATER SUPPLY ISSUES

SO FAR, we've looked at issues affecting water quality, from infrastructure-based lead contamination to industrial, agricultural, and accidental pollution. But water quality matters only if there is water to test in the first place.

Around the globe, there is significant distress about water quantity—especially with the increasing impact of climate change, which can lead to drought conditions. According to the World Health Organization an estimated 2.1 billion people throughout the world don't have access to an adequate drinking water supply.

The people affected live in developed and developing countries alike. Many are living through droughts. Others are dealing with poor management of a limited water source—including a community in New England, where the faucets suddenly ran dry.

CASE STUDY: HAMPSTEAD, NEW HAMPSHIRE— WHEN THE WELL RUNS DRY

When the well is dry, we'll know the worth of water.
—Benjamin Franklin, 1746, *Poor Richard's Almanack*

On a hot September afternoon in 2018, six-year-old Langdon Anthony bounded down the steps of his yellow school bus. He got a nod from his mom, and moments later, he was in his swim trunks, cooling off in the family pool. It wasn't the same as a bath, but it was refreshing, especially since there was no water flowing from the taps inside his family's New Hampshire house.

His mom, Deanna Anthony, recalled the day their house went dry. "It was a Monday morning," she said. "Everything was usual, and then I turned on the faucet. Nothing."

Just down the street from the Anthonys' home, the stars and stripes waved from the flagpole outside the Hampstead town hall. The colonial New England town of Hampstead, founded in 1749, incorporates old houses, a cemetery, war memorials, and a few stores. The Anthonys' home is one of the older houses. It has sat on the town's main street for over seventy-five years. Deanna and her husband, David Anthony, grew up in Hampstead and were happy to move back to the town as adults to raise Langdon.

"We moved here in May 2018," Deanna explained. "Our water was tested. It was flawless. It was one of the most beautiful water tests we've seen. It was almost too perfect. About a week and a half after we moved in, I turned on the faucet, and out came an orange sludge with the water. It was bubbly and filmy in the toilets. We still had plenty of water, though. We got busy with the move, and then about three weeks later, around July first, nothing came out."

When the taps went dry, Deanna Anthony checked the water tanks. There was no water pressure at all. It didn't make any sense. The family's water supply came from a newly drilled well. A new well should last many years, unless more water is drawn out of it than can be replenished with snow or rain.

By September 2018, the family was still without running water. The Anthonys were forced to rely on water from a refillable tank outside and a stash of donated jugs stored in their garage.

"Thank goodness for the pool," Deanna said. "I don't know what we'll do when we have to close it this fall." The pool served as a soapless bathing option during the hot summer. It wasn't an easy way for a family to live, let alone a family with an active six-year-old.

"If it's yellow, let it mellow. If it's brown, flush it down," young Langdon chimed in from the pool, reciting the water conservation saying by heart.

For the Anthonys, this rule wasn't merely an effort to conserve; it was a necessity. Each flush of a typical toilet uses between 1 and 6 gallons (4 and 23 liters) of water, depending on its age and design. The Anthonys didn't have that water to waste. Every time their tank was flushed, it needed refilling with expensive delivered water or precious donated water.

And the Anthonys weren't alone. Each of their neighbors had their own well, and many of them had also run dry.

What was happening? Deanna Anthony was determined to find out.

"Groundwater represents a bank. We can store water from decade to decade, and arguably millennium to millennium—but when we take a withdrawal from that bank, we have to hope there are deposits making up for our withdrawal. If there aren't deposits making up for the withdrawals, we have less water in the future to face water resource challenges with."
—Thomas Meixner, University of Arizona professor of hydrology and atmospheric sciences

PLAYING DETECTIVE

Deanna Anthony walked up and down the street, talking to her neighbors. She learned that about thirty homes had been impacted. Some of her neighbors needed to dig additional wells on their property in the hope of reaching another pocket of groundwater. The cost of drilling new wells runs into the thousands, however, and homeowners are responsible for the cost, not the town. Some neighbors feared losing their homes as the expenses grew.

The Anthonys called Skillings & Sons, the company that had dug their well. "At first, the well company thought it was a mechanical problem with the well itself," Deanna said. "Each time they came out, they believed it was a minor problem that could be fixed."

As the well company returned again and again, Deanna learned about the history of the property's wells. Before the Anthonys had moved in, it had taken Skillings & Sons three months

Deanna and Langdon Anthony were grateful for the donated jugs of water when their well ran dry.

to find a well site that would produce water. The third well they dug was the one that worked during the inspection process for the home prior to May 2018, when the Anthonys moved in.

But the story went even further back. Deanna discovered that the previous homeowner had dug four wells on the property over the course of the several years they'd lived in the house. Their first well produced plenty of water, but when a nearby apartment complex was built—meaning more people relying on the same limited supply of groundwater—another well had to be dug. As even more developments went up, the previous homeowner dug a third and then a fourth well. Could the increased number of people living in the area have strained Hamsptead's limited water resources? It seemed so as more wells ran dry.

Between 1980 and 1990, Hampstead's population increased from 3,785 to 6,848. By 2018, the population was 8,632. To accommodate the growth, new condominiums, apartments, and large single-family homes were built throughout the town.

In the summer of 2018, new residential construction was happening just up the road from the Anthonys' house. Blasting and well drilling was underway for four new houses, and six more homes were planned for the same street. That meant a total of ten new wells drawing water from the same underground aquifer as the Anthonys and their neighbors.

But the new home construction wasn't the whole story. After further investigation, Deanna learned that Hampstead Area Water Company (HAWC), the supplier of municipal water for thirty-seven hundred homes in thirteen towns of southern New Hampshire, had drilled about twenty commercial wells throughout their town. An April 2019 report by the New Hampshire Department of Environmental Services (NHDES) connected the homeowners' lack of water to excessive pumping at one of the HAWC's wells, located at Kent Farm.

No Water, No Value

Like Flint, Michigan, and Hoosick, New York, residents, the Anthonys discovered that homes lose all their value if they don't have clean, potable water. Just as new homes were being built near the Anthonys', the area's existing houses were becoming worthless. "Our house is worth zero dollars right now, after paying full price for it just a few months ago," said Deanna in early fall of 2018.

CITIZEN ADVOCATES

A year after their water problems began, the Anthonys and their neighbors formed Hampstead Water Advocates. They held town meetings and worked on legislation to protect their groundwater supply. They also investigated the current HAWC wells. Deanna learned that the company's Kent Farm well field was pumping over 100 gallons (379 liters) per *minute* out of the aquifer. That translates to a lot more water than the average home requires. An average American family uses roughly 300 gallons (1,136 liters) per day.

"You're taking our water which nobody produces—God produces it—and you're taking it, and you're using it as a resource to sell," said Joe Guthrie, a Republican state representative from Hampstead, at a 2019 hearing about HAWC's practices. "We think we should have some benefit from it."

After the NHDES report linking the HAWC Kent Farm well to the residential water shortages, the Hampstead homeowners filed a lawsuit. In January 2021, Rockingham County Superior Court Judge Daniel St. Hilaire ruled that the Hampstead Area Water Company must not pump more than 35 gallons (132 liters) per minute from the Kent Farm well field. The ruling also required the water company to provide a minimum of 400 gallons (1,514 liters) per day to David and Deanna Anthony's residence for the duration of the civil case litigation. That was great news for the Anthonys after such a long battle.

But water issues don't resolve overnight. It sometimes takes years, though there can be successes along the way. For example, after forming Hampstead Water Advocates, Deanna Anthony worked to get two articles on the local ballot in 2019. Article 4 asked voters to strengthen requirements for well permits and provide water flow test reports to building inspectors. It was voted in 1,950 to 298. Article 22, titled "Preserve Groundwater," asked local officials, known in New England as selectmen, to use federal, town, county, and state funds to preserve and protect the town's groundwater, investigate alternate sources of public water to supplement the town's groundwater, and scrutinize zoning ordinances to protect and preserve water quantity and quality. It passed by a vote of 2,023 to 253. While Deanna struggled with her family's water, she's made an enormous difference in her town. ◌

Voices Raised

Deanna Anthony wasn't the only one raising her voice in Hampstead. When a 2018 school assignment required her to write a letter to local legislators about an important topic, fifteen-year-old honor student Alexandrine Lacasse chose Hampstead's water crisis as her topic. It was an issue she knew firsthand—her friends and family were among those in the homes without water. Lacasse went straight to the top, sending her letter to the governor of New Hampshire, Chris Sununu. She wrote: "There is only so much a group can do when everyone around them brushes them off and says they need to deal with it themselves, sir." When she didn't receive a reply, Lacasse called the statehouse in Concord and found herself connected to the governor himself. Governor Sununu had read the letter and informed Lacasse that he had sent an inquiry to the New Hampshire Department of Environmental Services, which ended up filing the 2019 report linking the HAWC commercial wells to the water shortage.

Robert Frost in Hampstead

Although this particular problem in Hampstead was due to excess water pumped out by the local water company, New Hampshire's water table can also be affected by times of drought. Even the famous poet Robert Frost, who once lived just up the road from the Anthonys, had a problem one dry summer. He wrote the poem "Going for Water," in 1913, about heading to a brook to get water when the well at his house ran dry.

WATER SHORTAGE IS A GLOBAL ISSUE

The lack of water in Hampstead, New Hampshire, shows us that we shouldn't take our water supply for granted. It also highlights the danger of having too many people or companies drawing from the same limited water resources, depleting the groundwater supply faster than it can be naturally replenished.

While having too many straws in the milkshake is a problem in some areas, many other US households—roughly 460,000—are struggling with a total lack of a plumbing connection to fresh water.

And the lack of water isn't just a problem in the United States—it's global. Climate change is only making the situation more difficult, especially in areas that are already dry. Some of these regions now face multiyear droughts that push water availability to the brink. In some places, like South Africa, people are counting down the days until they completely run out of water.

CASE STUDY: CAPE TOWN, SOUTH AFRICA— DAY ZERO

April 12, 2018. That was the predicted day Cape Town, South Africa, would run out of water. Unlike the small community of Hampstead, New Hampshire, this water shortage would affect a city of four million people.

South Africa is one of the thirty most water-scarce countries in the world. The Day Zero prediction was made following three years of severe drought caused, at least in part, by the warming climate. The city's growing population, overdevelopment, and increased water use were also factors. There were fewer resources serving more people: Between 2014 and 2015, water levels held in the city's dams decreased from 71.9 percent to 50.1 percent.

City officials began their countdown to Day Zero in January 2018, three months away from the predicted doomsday. Even though officials made strides in reducing the use of water by charging large users more, fixing leaks in the infrastructure, and promoting water efficiency, the efforts weren't enough.

As the city prepped for Day Zero, it planned for two hundred emergency water stations to be set up outside grocery stores and other spots in the city. Each station would serve close to twenty thousand Cape Town residents. It became illegal for residents to use water to fill up pools, wash cars, or water gardens. The city also established patrols to guard against theft at natural springs.

With heightened fear and determination, the people of Cape Town rallied. Residents lowered their personal water consumption. Restrictions were put in place to limit the amount of water to 13 gallons (50 liters) per day per person, an amount that wouldn't even cover the average American's single, eight-minute shower, which uses over 17 gallons (64 liters) of water.

Cape Town residents had to break down those fifty liters in a way that addressed all their water needs, which included everything from cooking, bathing, and drinking to toilet flushes, dog bowl filling, and brushing teeth.

It was a huge challenge, but everyone changed the way they lived to avoid the looming catastrophe. They harvested any available rainwater in cisterns and barrels to use for washing and other nondrinking essential uses. This enabled them to decrease their use of municipal water, keeping the levels of the city's six major reservoirs as high as possible.

Their efforts paid off. Thanks to the decrease in consumption and the oncoming rains, which would help refill the reservoirs, Capetonians were able to push Day Zero off for at least another year. But this wasn't a long-term solution.

"Indications are that our rainfall patterns are getting harder to predict," said Lindiwe Sisulu, the minister of Human Settlements, Water and Sanitation in a 2019 Reuters interview. "What we're seeing, like other parts of the globe, is the dry season is getting longer, harsher and more intense. Climate change is a reality and is affecting South Africa."

The city set up a website called Water Dashboard where residents and others could view the daily water-use target versus the actual use as well as the percentage of water held in the city's dams. In June 2020, the daily water-use target was 172 million gallons (651 million liters), while the actual use was 193 million gallons (731 million liters). They had a little more work to do to hit their target. But as the residents were working on their water consumption, the dams began to fill.

As of November 1, 2020, Cape Town was celebrating dams filled to capacity and zero water restrictions. From Day Zero to zero restrictions was indeed cause for celebration. While they have managed to avoid Day Zero, Cape Town residents are now more fully aware of their water consumption and how to manage themselves if they experience that water stress again. 💧

DAY ZERO RISK AROUND THE WORLD

The problem of water scarcity isn't just Cape Town's—other cities around the globe are at risk of reaching Day Zero, too. Tokyo, London, São Paulo, Beijing, Bangalore, and Los Angeles also face tremendous water shortages.

Notably, Chennai, India, faced a similar crisis to Cape Town in 2019 when local reservoirs, including Chembarambakkam Lake, ran dry. Fingers pointed to local industry and development. Similar to America's Detroit, Chennai has many car manufacturers, all requiring water for power to run their machines. It's also a technology hub. These industries were outstripping the supply of water in the area. By the middle of 2020, Chennai was in better shape, thanks to planning and a little luck. The lakes supplying the city were fuller, and the city had reduced the use of fresh water in industrial areas by supplying them with recycled water.

But if water management issues and climate change's warming temperatures continue to challenge these cities, Day Zero risks will only increase. And it's not just humans who are impacted. Animals suffer, too. As climate change brings more drought, wildlife must search for water resources that often don't exist. This can lead to mass population deaths that threaten species survival. Many of these tragic losses have happened in Australia, one of the world's driest continents and a hub of natural biodiversity.

CASE STUDY: AUSTRALIA— A WATER CRISIS DOWN UNDER

In November 2018, the temperature rose to a record-breaking 42 degrees Celsius (108 degrees Fahrenheit) in northern Australia. The heat killed vegetation and caused the streets to melt. Every living thing suffered.

In just two days, an estimated twenty-three thousand spectacled flying foxes, a species of fruit-eating megabat that pollinates local trees, perished. Residents in Cairns in Queensland saw their treasured local megabats falling from their tree

Megabats, like this spectacled flying fox in Cairns, Australia, cannot survive extreme droughts and heat waves. According to the International Union for Conservation of Nature (IUCN), their risk of extinction increased from threatened to endangered in 2020.

perches into swimming pools, backyards, and seaside streets. It was frightening and heartbreaking. Roughly a third of the flying foxes in Australia were lost, and some ecologists think the toll was even higher.

The flying fox wasn't the only species afflicted. The heat sparked wildfires, which raged through dry areas and caused the deaths of koala bears and numerous other threatened species. And as the record-breaking temperatures and intense drought caused water levels to drop and water to heat up, fish suffered, too. In January 2019, the country's single hottest month on record, hundreds of thousands of fish died in just a matter of days. In New South Wales, a white carpet of dead fish covered the Darling River, a critical waterway that millions rely on for food and drinking water.

Farmers have also experienced catastrophic deaths of livestock Down Under. Australians are accustomed to hot, dry conditions, and dangerous droughts, like the Millennium Drought in southeastern Australia dating from late 1996 into 2010. But the recurring droughts since 2012 have been the hottest on record, bringing death to cattle ranches, sheep farms, and vast areas of crops. Drought and heat have also killed off grazing grass, requiring farmers to truck in expensive feed to keep their animals alive. Dry, hot conditions have also weakened animals, many of which have ventured off into creekbeds and gotten trapped in the drying mud, died in the shade of the few trees surviving, or been attacked by crows and monitor lizards.

The deaths weighed on everyone. Jack Slack-Smith, a farmer in New South Wales, lost over 3,000 of his herd of 7,000 sheep. Most of his herd of breeding cattle also perished, reduced from 260 to only 22.

If changes in water management and allocation don't occur, Australians are likely to see these problems continue, particularly as the effects of climate change intensify. ◊

"No matter how hard you work,
you still can't make it rain."
—Jim Skinner, an Australian farmer

CHAPTER 8: HELL OR HIGH WATER— FLOODING AND SEA LEVEL RISE

ANYONE WHO IS SUFFERING IN AN AREA OF WATER SCARCITY would find it hard to imagine being inundated with water, but this is a reality for many people around the globe as climate change has made wet regions wetter. While our warming climate brings severe droughts to some regions, it also causes heightened storms and rising seas, both of which can leave more water in their wake than can be handled.

Too much water is as dangerous as too little. What happens to communities that suffer from an overabundance of water? Let's take a look at the Isle de Jean Charles in Louisiana, where rising seas are forcing residents to become climate refugees.

CASE STUDY: ISLE DE JEAN CHARLES, LOUISIANA— AN ISLAND'S CLIMATE REFUGEES

The state of Louisiana has been losing thousands of acres of land into the rising sea since the 1930s. And now faster than ever. In the three hours it takes for you to watch a professional football game on television, two football field-sized pieces of land have slipped into the ocean from Louisiana and the Mississippi Delta. And there aren't many places in Louisiana that have been affected more seriously than the tiny barrier island of Isle de Jean Charles, located about eighty miles southwest of New Orleans.

The island once covered thousands of acres and was about the size of the island of Manhattan. By 2018 it had decreased by 98 percent. Once a home to three hundred families, by February 2019, only twenty families were still calling it home. The island was listed on the Cultural Landscape Foundation's *Landslide 2019: Living in Nature* report as an area threatened to be forever compromised or destroyed by climate change. In recent years, the island's shrinking land mass has been accelerated by a devastating series of hurricanes, including Hurricane Barry.

In July 2019, Barry swept across the Gulf of Mexico and into Louisiana, slamming Louisiana's barrier islands, which were already suffering from rising sea levels, offshore oil spills, and poverty. It was a category 1 hurricane—not the strongest by far, but it was enough to put the two-mile-long, quarter-mile-wide island of Isle de Jean Charles over the edge.

A dozen residents on the island had to be rescued from Barry's high waters, which rose ten to fifteen feet overnight. Eight people were rescued by the US Coast Guard. Four others were rescued with their cat from a roof by helicopter basket.

In the wake of Hurricane Barry, the members of the Biloxi-Chitimacha-Choctaw tribe who lived on Isle de Jean Charles knew that their Mississippi Delta island would probably not survive another hurricane. Still, it was difficult for them to leave the place that had been home to their tribal family for centuries.

"I always talk about water as our life and our death.
The water that sustains us and provides for us is killing us."
—Chantel Comardelle, Biloxi-Chitimacha-Choctaw
executive secretary

ISLAND HISTORY

The Chitimacha tribe inhabited the barrier islands in Terrebonne Parish, Louisiana, for a thousand years before Europeans arrived. They grew corn, beans, melons, and squash. They hunted and fished. They created baskets from river cane.

After Columbus and other Europeans arrived, the tribe suffered from measles, smallpox, and other illnesses brought by the foreigners. Their numbers decreased from around twenty thousand to roughly four thousand. A war with the French in the early 1700s resulted in more casualties. Survivors moved north in the Mississippi Delta to an island known as Isle de Jean Charles. There they lived peacefully for years.

In the 1830s, the Indian Removal Act forced the relocation of many tribes, including the Indigenous peoples of the south—the Choctaw, Chickasaw, and Muscogee—along the Trail of Tears. To avoid relocation, many of these people fled into the Delta for safety and made Isle de Jean Charles their home, living alongside the people already there.

Over the years, the residents of the island peaceably survived while farming the land and fishing the waters—until the sea arrived.

NO MORE FARMING

According to Chantel Comardelle, executive secretary for the Biloxi-Chitimacha-Choctaw of Louisiana, there used to be "massive amounts of gardens, cattle, lots of livestock" on the island. But the island has seen a loss of land and a sea level rise since 1955. As climate change caused glaciers to melt and the sea to rise, the rising sea brought salt water and erosion to the island, making the soil too salty to be farmed. The salinity in the soil killed off all the island's bald cypresses, live oak trees, and farmland. Household gardens were raised to protect them from the damaging flow of salt. The effort worked for the short term, but there were other problems with the rising waters. High tides carried pollution from offshore oil spills to the shores. The raised garden beds weren't enough to protect the vegetables from the toxic seawater. Flooded yards became typical, even during normal high tides.

Farming wasn't the only problem. The waters surrounding the island once supplied a rich bounty of seafood. But diminishing quantities of fish, caused by commercial overfishing and the offshore oil spills, could not sustain the residents anymore.

As the island continued to lose land and food sources and face a series of hard-hitting hurricanes, its residents had to

Island Drinking Water

In addition to the threats posed by rising seas, island residents also faced contamination of their drinking water. A spigot for drinking water on the island is located on the outside of a levee. Residents still living on the island in 2018 kept it on all the time so the water would keep dripping and remain free from harmful bacteria. And not just any bacteria. In 2018, a brain-eating amoeba called *Naegleria fowleri* was confirmed in the Terrebonne Parish water system for the third time in three years. According to the US Centers for Disease Control and Prevention, this contamination leads to an infection that begins with headaches, fever, and nausea. If left unchecked, it then progresses to hallucinations, loss of balance, and seizures. Although it is rare, the infection is almost always deadly. Because of the contamination, island residents have been forced to rely on bottled water.

Island Road, Isle de Jean Charles, flooded following Hurricane Laura in 2020.

decide whether or not to leave their homes and join the growing number of climate refugees—people who must move when
climate change threatens their land—all around the world.

RELOCATION

Where do people go when the sea has gobbled up their homes?
And even if they can figure out where to go, how do they afford
to move? Like so many other communities that have felt the
impact of a water crisis, Isle de Jean Charles residents were
faced with the fact that their homes had no resale value. There
would be no money from a house sale to put toward a down
payment on another home.

And if they did move, how could their tribe stay connected? Starting in the early 2000s, after two back-to-back
hurricanes, the tribal council of the island began struggling

with the decision to relocate the tribe to mainland Louisiana. Some members had already moved on their own. But Albert Naquin, chief of the Biloxi-Chitimacha-Choctaw Indians, was concerned that once the tribal members became scattered in different areas, they would lose their community and culture. Unlike the families in Flint, Newark, or Hoosick that could relocate separately to another area, these families belonged to a tribal community. A treaty granted them their land. Moving to nontribal land would affect their way of life, their connection to the land, and their continuity.

The tribe worked for nearly twenty years to find affordable, sustainable housing, striving for total tribal resettlement on higher, drier land to keep their community together. Members testified in May 2016 to the US House Natural Resources Committee to garner support for their resettlement plans.

"We knew we had to ensure our future," Chantal Comardelle said. "We want people to be safe and have a rich life."

The tribe won a grant of $48 million for its resettlement from the Louisiana's Office of Community Development. The new location, about 40 miles (64 kilometers) north on land once used for growing sugarcane, would not be considered official tribal land, as the island has been. But it was higher, drier, and could fit the tribe. It would include wetlands, bayous, orchards, a fishing pond, a solar farm, pastureland, and homes.

Isle de Jean Charles residents had until the end of January 2020 to apply for a home in the new housing development or for an existing home somewhere else in Louisiana through the state's Office of Community Development. But for many, the loss of tribal land meant the loss of their tribal identity, and without a cultural center or place for a powwow in their new mainland community, only half the families on the island considered relocating.

One of the tribal members who chose to stay on the island in his house on 12-foot (3.6-meter) stilts after Hurricane Katrina, Edison Dardar Jr. posted this sign: "We are not moving off the island. If some people want to move, they can go. But leave us alone. The people have the right to live where they want, not where people tell them to go and live. They say the island is fading away. Soon we will not have an island left. If the island is not good, stay away. May God bless the island."

Juliette Brunet (Choctaw) is a sixteen-year-old who was still living on the island in 2020. She and her older brother, Howard, are featured in the 2019 documentary short *Lowland Kids: Growing Up on a Disappearing Island*. She's watched the island over the years as the houses have tilted into the bayous and water has flooded her family's island home. Like many other teens, Juliette worries about climate change. She and her brother are the only teens remaining on Isle de Jean Charles. They know what is to come, and they are choosing to add their voices to the choir of other youth activists across the globe. ⬩

RISING SEAS AROUND THE WORLD

The Isle de Jean Charles community helped create a tool kit called *A Community Field Guide to Engagement, Resilience, and Resettlement*. Residents knew that although they were among the world's first climate refugees needing to move away from their homes due to sea level rise, they would not be the last.

The National Oceanic and Atmospheric Administration reports that sea level has risen about 9 inches (23 cm) since 1880 and is still rising. This rise—along with intensifying storms, which are also tied to climate change—is affecting many other areas both within and outside the United States. In 2017, Hurricane Maria displaced an estimated twenty-three hundred Puerto Rican families. In 2020, more than a dozen coastal communities in Alaska were working on relocating due to rising seas. Pacific Island nations such as Samoa and Fiji faced a similar threat.

And across the Atlantic, the famous and historic city of Venice, Italy, is also facing a sea-level crisis years in the making.

CASE STUDY: VENICE, ITALY—EMPLOYING TECHNOLOGY TO SAVE A CITY

There are 150 canals flowing through Venice, Italy, a city that celebrated its 1600th anniversary in 2021.

In October 2018, locals and tourists pulled on rain boots to trek through the city of Venice's Piazza San Marco (St. Mark's Square), a place Napoléon I called "the most beautiful drawing room in Europe." Floodwater had risen above the piazza and right into the square's famous Caffè Florian, open since 1720. "The parquet flooring lifted right up," the hostess said in 2018. "The only time that has happened since the 1950s."

Just two months after that record flood, the waters had subsided. St. Mark's Piazza was dry, decorated for Christmas, and walkable. But everyone still talked about the flooding. And then another flood arrived in November 2019 that dwarfed the one the year before. Two people died as the water level rose to the highest level in over fifty years, flooding more than 85 percent of the city. As water poured into shops and homes, power sockets short-circuited, plunging buildings into darkness and causing water pumps to stop.

Luca Zaia, Veneto region governor, described the 2019 flooding as "apocalyptic devastation." Mayor Luigi Brugnaro tweeted that his city was "on its knees."

THE HIGH TIDES

Venice, where canals flow in lieu of streets, has always experienced periodic flooding from high tides, known in Italian as *acqua alta*. But because of sea level rise, the high tides are becoming more frequent and more destructive. Between 1960 and 1970, there were three extreme flood events in Venice. There were only two in the next decade. But there have been two per year in 2009, 2012, and 2018.

With each high tide, the canal walls and parts of historic buildings become submerged for hours at a time. When the tide goes out, it leaves behind wet, salt-covered bricks. The salt slowly eats away at the clay. If this pattern of flooding continues, the bricks will eventually turn into powder.

Raised walkways accommodate Venetians and visitors in the high water, but they don't help the city structures. After a flood, some property owners hose down the bricks of their buildings with fresh water to slow the damage. But it's impossible to hose down an entire city.

THE MOSE PROJECT

Venice and its lagoon were designated a UNESCO World Heritage site in 1987, meaning the city has significant importance to world culture. It is filled with outstanding art and architecture from the Renaissance period that has inspired the world for over five hundred years. It draws 26 million to 30 million visitors annually.

Will the tides eventually consume this historic city? City managers are working to see that they don't, using a highly engineered flood barrier system called MOSE. The acronym stands for Modulo Sperimentale Elettromeccanico (Experimental Electromechanical Module); it is also a nod to Moses, who is said to have parted the seas.

The MOSE project is Venice's version of the Thames Barrier that prevents central London from being flooded; it involves four defense mobile barriers, composed of twenty-one gates, that act as retractable floodgates. They can be raised and lowered across the mouths of the historic city's three lagoon inlets to help ward against dangerous flooding. Officials and residents hope these barriers, along with other climate change mitigation efforts, will help prevent future flooding and preserve the city.

The MOSE project started in 2003 and was scheduled for completion in 2014, but that endpoint was moved out to the end of 2021. Residents and environmental scientists fear that it might be obsolete. The design, over twenty years old now, may not be enough to counter the fast rise in sea level. The world is still at risk of losing this valuable historical city. Venice residents may one day join other climate refugees around the world in search of a new, drier home. 💧

COOPERATION IS KEY

How far above sea level do you live? Coastal cities from Venice to Miami have experienced the brunt of sea level rise, but you don't have to live on a coast to be affected. As more people move from those areas inland to higher ground, and as the coastal farmland that feeds us floods with salty seas and becomes unproductive, we'll all feel the effects of sea level rise.

Measures are being taken to mitigate these scenarios. Salt-resistant crops are being explored, for instance, along with various measures to keep the water at bay. To survive, cities like Venice will have to learn from each other how to combat sea level rise, flooding, and storms due to climate change. Like any element of the global water crisis—whether it's a water quality or quantity issue—cooperation between people, communities, and nations is essential for effective problem solving.

Sadly, humans don't always work together in harmony when facing a loss of resources.

While heightened water stress can lead to cooperation, it can also lead to conflict, as we'll explore next. 💧

CHAPTER 9: CONFLICT AND COOPERATION—HOW WATER STRESS AFFECTS NATIONS

ISSUES WITH CONTAMINATED WATER, too little water, or too much water have caused water stress in nations and communities around the world. In 2018, senior military officers summed up the situation: "With escalating global population and the impact of a changing climate, we see the challenges of water stress rising with time." The officers were from CNA, a nonprofit research and analysis organization working on America's national security. The United Nations, meanwhile, claims that by 2025, two-thirds of the world will be surviving under "water-stressed" conditions.

This water stress sometimes leads to conflict, particularly in regions also dealing with water mismanagement and political instability. Water conflicts can take the form of territorial disputes, separatist movements, contested governments, and ethnic and religious divisions. CNA issued a 2018 report on global water stress, stating: "Freshwater is so vital to the human condition, conventional wisdom holds that populations would be willing to go to war to ensure supplies."

According to Julia McQuaid, principal research scientist at CNA, there is a pattern that occurs with a water-stressed society. First, there's civil unrest. People start to become tense, and little skirmishes might develop. If the water stress isn't resolved, local violence can follow, and it will only become worse if the situation isn't corrected. That could take the form of terrorism, insurgencies, and even civil wars or all-out warfare between countries.

In the news, we hear daily reports of conflicts in desert countries of the Middle East. Delving into these hostilities often reveals water stress as one of the reasons for the escalating tensions.

CASE STUDY: IRAN—DESERTIFICATION TURNS GOOD LAND BAD

Iran is one country on track for extreme water scarcity as the climate continues to warm, the population grows, and available water decreases. According to Claudia Sadoff, a water specialist who reported with World Bank's Water Global Practice consultant Edoardo Borgomeo on Iran's water crisis for the World Bank's report *Beyond Scarcity: Water Security in the Middle East and North Africa*: "Twenty-five percent of the total water withdrawn from aquifers, rivers, and lakes exceeds the amount that can be replenished."

As agriculture diverts more and more water from rivers and streams, Iran's eastern and southern regions will become barren and face desertification. A true desert ecosystem teems with desert plants and wildlife. It has a delicate balance of soil nutrients and water. Desertification is different—it occurs when the soil changes, rain can no longer penetrate it, and it can no longer support life. This kind of land degradation can result from a variety of factors, including a changing climate and human activities like overfarming and wasteful water practices. In Iran's case, drought, overgrazing, fire, and defor-estation are also contributors.

The head of Iran's Environmental Department, Issa Kalantari, spoke about the future of his country and desertifi-cation in 2017. At a ceremony celebrating World Soil Day, he warned, "If water consumption for agriculture remains at this level, in less than twenty-five years Iran's eastern and south-ern areas will be completely deserted, and fifty million people will have to emigrate." He added: "90 percent to 95 percent of water consumed in the agricultural sector must be reduced; otherwise, the problem will never be solved." According to Iran's Forests, Range and Watershed Management Organization, 247 million acres (100 million hectares) of land are threatened.

"Iran is one example of water stress triggering unrest on the low end, whether those are riots, protests or strikes," CNA's Julia McQuaid said in Flint, Michigan, in 2018. And this water stress doesn't end at the human-made border.

Iran's neighbor Afghanistan shares the same weather and the same water sources. Melting snows in Afghanistan flow into rivers that cross into Iran and Pakistan. The three coun-tries have disputed over water access for decades. And the water supply is now dwindling. Frequent droughts and hotter temperatures mean less rain and snowfall and more evapora-tion from existing water bodies. In the few years leading up to 2018, the water levels in the region dropped by 13 billion cubic yards (10 billion cubic meters)—a devastating amount for local farmers.

A 1973 treaty between Iran and Afghanistan set out a plan for sharing the waters of the Helmand River with farmers. But each side claims the other is using more than they should. Iran points to two hydroelectric dams that Afghanistan built on the river. Afghanistan claims that decades of war with Iran has made it impossible to properly measure the river's outtake across the border.

The two countries are attempting to work together to set up a new water measurement station at the border where the river crosses into Iran. Although these countries have other important resources, like coal and iron, nothing is more valuable in a dry country than water. 💧

Syria's Tipping Point

Another country suffering from water stress is Syria, on the shore of the Mediterranean Sea. Syria experienced a devastating drought from 2006 to 2010. As fields died, farmers abandoned their farms in search of other work to earn money to feed their families. They migrated to cities in the hope of finding employment. But not everyone could find jobs. The country was already experiencing political unrest, and the lack of water was a tipping point. The water stress led to hostilities that fueled the country's civil war.

India's Water Mafia

In the slums of Delhi, India, there aren't enough water pipes to service the area's 30 million people. The government brings in water tankers once a week to provide the residents with water, but a weekly delivery isn't enough for most families.

This stress created an opportunity for the so-called water mafia to develop a black market for water. These men illegally dig deep wells, then pump water from the wells and into waiting tankers. They sell it back to residents at a high cost. The residents scrounge what little money they have to pay for water while they wait for the annual monsoon rains to come and alleviate their thirst.

Besides charging high prices for their black-market water, the water mafia also employs the same strong-arm tactics as other organized crime networks. They make threats—and violently carry them out. In 2018, a TV reporter was kidnapped and beaten by the water mafia for attempting to report on their criminal activity.

India's sacred yet highly polluted Ganges River is threatened with water loss stemming from climate change and groundwater depletion.

Causes for Hope

Water stress poses a dangerous threat to world stability, and it can be exacerbated by other global events. This was the case with the COVID-19 pandemic when hand washing became a lifesaving measure. Places suffering from lack of water, like Delhi, India. for example, faced lockdown in 2020 without enough water for residents. Making matters worse, some water suppliers stopped operating in Delhi during the pandemic, while others inflated prices. Other communities without clean water—like Flint,

Michigan; Hoosick, New York; and the Navajo Nation reservation—also face increased hardship during events like the 2020 pandemic. The United Nations reports that the lack of water and sanitation during the pandemic exacerbated violence against women and girls in countries, like Yemen, where they often must travel alone for two to four hours each day to collect water.

Fortunately, there are causes for hope. Programs around the world—many sponsored by the United Nations—are offering relief to communities suffering from water stress. In Delhi, for instance, organizations like WaterAid and FORCE have helped install taps in people's homes. And while water stress often leads to conflict, we've also seen that it can sometimes bring nations together.

CASE STUDY: AFGHANISTAN—NATIONS COME TOGETHER TO MANAGE WATER STRESS

Kabul be zar basha be barf ne!
—Ancient Persian saying that translates to:
"May Kabul be without gold rather than snow."

The snowpack on the Hindu Kush mountains near the city of Kabul is more precious than glittering gold. Afghanistan's agriculture and people depend on it. About 80 percent of the country's water flows from glaciers and snowpack from the Hindu Kush and Himalaya mountain ranges into five river basins. The water then travels into canals and throughout the country.

Like its Middle East neighbors, Afghanistan faces climate challenges that are creating water stress. Hotter winters and more torrential spring rains have changed the rhythm and flow of Afghanistan's water resources. Higher temperatures have caused earlier snowmelt each year, and much of that water doesn't sink into the cracked soil to feed plants and recharge the groundwater. Instead, it's lost as runoff. There are also more flash floods and droughts. Afghanistan experienced a decline of 1.4 millimeters in groundwater level between 2004 and 2012 and a 62 percent drop in annual rainfall in 2018 due to climate change.

But climate change isn't the only cause of the country's water crisis. Decades of war and mismanagement of water resources have also been detrimental. War destroyed much of the country's canals, many of them underground channels for irrigation. In addition, the country's Ministry of Energy and Water reports that 90 percent of its water resources are being used for agriculture rather than drinking and other household uses. More cooperation and management are needed.

THE WATER MASTERS

For thousands of years, Mirabs have monitored irrigation systems in the region. These traditional water masters or water guardians are elected by local councils and paid by landowners. They practice a mixture of ancient tribal laws, Islamic laws, and modern laws to resolve local water disputes, determine water rights, and help farmers plan irrigation for their land. Roughly 65 percent of Afghanistan's irrigation systems are operated by Mirabs. The water masters spend much of their days walking along the irrigation canals to inspect and control structures. If an irrigation canal is long, multiple people maintain sections. But as useful as this system has been over the centuries, it faces challenges.

Some Mirabs in the western region of Afghanistan still use the *Taximot Hakobe Ab*, a fifteenth-century text by Abdul Rahman Jami. It gives detailed instructions for irrigation designs and calculations for the flow of water. This critical text is not, however, readily available. Most villagers don't have access to it. This is coupled with the problem that many Mirabs are not trained in modern agricultural irrigation practices, which are often expensive—the increasing costs of fertilizer, insecticides, pesticides, seeds, and machinery are limiting the funds available for hiring Mirabs. The water masters can also have trouble standing up to powerful people acting as warlords. They can be easily threatened.

Outdated water management and engineering plans make it impossible for Afghanistan to use its water resources efficiently. As a result, it needs help from other countries. The US Army Corps of Engineers assessed ways to bring water to the Afghan people in 2010. US hydrologists helped with the plans by examining the conditions in all the provinces and choosing five sites that could be used for hydropower and to recharge the groundwater. Building dams on these sites would not only help with the country's water management but would also provide important employment opportunities.

This was not the first time the United States helped with Afghanistan's water management. In 1952, the country's Arghandab River reservoir was completed with the US-funded earthen Dahla Dam. The dam originally held 83 billion gallons (314 billion liters) of water, but over the decades it was neglected and fell into ruin. In 2014, the US Army Corps of Engineers returned to repair it and increase the reservoir's capacity.

"Water is life. This water will help everyone in the region," Danielle Lovellette, the Corps's project engineer, stated in a 2014 US Army press release. The Dahla Dam repair was scheduled for completion in 2017, but the date was pushed back to 2024 because of political issues.

The United States isn't alone in helping Afghanistan. The country has also received help from Canada, Turkey, and India, among other countries.

THE AFGHAN-INDIA FRIENDSHIP DAM

The Afghanistan-India Friendship Dam—a hydroelectric and irrigation dam in the western province of Herat, Afghanistan—began with a feasibility plan in 1957, but the Soviet invasion of Afghanistan in 1979 halted the project. Continued instability in the country led to years of delay. There were even Iranian and Taliban plots to blow up the dam.

Then, in 2006, neighboring India invested in the project. The dam was inaugurated on June 4, 2016, by Indian Prime Minister Narendra Modi and Afghan President Ashraf Ghani. At the inauguration in Herat, Modi said, "We are reviving a region, restoring hope, renewing life and redefining Afghanistan's future. The dam is a generator not just of electricity but also of optimism and belief in the future of Afghanistan."

The specs for the $300 million dam, built on the Hari River, are impressive. It irrigates the fields of 640 villages (75,000 hectares, about 185,329 acres) and generates 42 megawatts of power to bring light to over 250,000 homes. ⬤

WATER IS A HUMAN RIGHT

The partnerships between Afghanistan, the United States, Canada, Turkey, and India demonstrate that cooperation between countries can help alleviate water stress. In 2010, the United Nations laid the groundwork for recognizing the importance of water and providing much more global cooperation.

On June 17, 2010, the United Nation's ambassador of Bolivia, Pablo Solón Romero, walked into a closed-door meeting at the UN General Assembly to make a bold proposal. He proposed a declaration—the human right to "available, safe, acceptable, accessible and affordable water and sanitation."

It was the first time the General Assembly, made up of representatives from nations around the world, would confront the issue of global water availability. Romero was already an activist, having worked on behalf of human rights and other social causes in Bolivia. He had also spearheaded resolutions at the UN on the Rights of Indigenous Peoples, International Mother Earth Day, and Harmony with Nature. He knew that declaring water a human right was important, not only for his country but for all countries.

The following month, Romero stood in front of the General Assembly to present the water resolution to the world. Backing him were close to forty co-sponsoring countries, including many tiny island nations that had already felt the impact of rising seas, like Samoa, Haiti, Cuba, and Fiji. There were others, too, that had felt water stress: Saudi Arabia, Ecuador, Nicaragua, and Yemen.

"Allow me to begin the presentation of this resolution by recalling that human beings are essentially water," Romero said to the United Nations members sitting behind their nameplates in the large assembly room.

He continued, "Around two-thirds of our organism is comprised of water. Some 75 percent of our brain is made up of water, and water is the principal vehicle for the electrochemical transmissions of our body. Our blood flows like a network of rivers in our body. Blood helps transport nutrients and energy to our organism. Water also carries from our cells waste products for excretion. Water helps to regulate the temperature of our body. The loss of 20 percent of body water can cause death. It is possible to survive for various weeks without food, but it is not possible to survive more than a few days without water. Water is life."

He also described the fate of human existence without clean water and sanitation: "This is why we, the co-sponsors, present this resolution in order that we now recognize the human right to water and sanitation, at a time when illness caused by lack of drinking water and sanitation causes more deaths than does war. Every year, three and a half million people die of waterborne illness. Diarrhea is the second-largest cause of death among children under five. The lack of access to potable water kills more children than AIDS, malaria, and smallpox combined. Worldwide, approximately one in eight people lack potable water. In just one day, more than two hundred million hours of women's time is consumed by collecting and transporting water for domestic use. The situation of lack of sanitation is far worse, for it affects 2.6 billion people, or 40 percent of the global population."

The ambassador reminded everyone of basic rights listed in the UN's Universal Declaration of Human Rights, including the right to an education, the right to work, and the right to rest. But it did not include the right to clean water. To him, the question was obvious: Why not declare something so fundamental to our well-being as water?

"The right to drinking water and sanitation are independent rights that should be recognized as such," he said. "It is not sufficient to urge states to comply with their human rights obligations relative to access to drinking water and sanitation. Instead, it is necessary to call on states to promote and protect the human right to drinking water and sanitation."

He concluded with this horrific fact: "24,000 children die in developing countries every day from preventable causes like diarrhea contracted from unclean water. That is one child death every three and a half seconds. One, two, three . . . As my people say, 'Now is the time.'"

The UN secretary called for a vote, and the resolution passed on July 28, 2010. It declares "the right to safe and clean drinking water and sanitation as a human right that is essential for the full enjoyment of life and all human rights," and called upon the global community of nations and organizations to use their resources to help provide "safe, clean, accessible and affordable drinking water and sanitation for all."

TAKING IT FORWARD

What does it mean for water to be a human right, and how do we achieve this goal? According to the UN, having agreed upon the human right to clean water and sanitation, countries must now invest money and other resources to make it a global reality.

A UN declaration is an expression of sentiments, however, and is not binding on any government. It's up to national and local governments to decide how to administer water rights, and so far, laws have not universally supported the UN's proclamation. And not all countries voted for the UN resolution. Some countries abstained out of fear that countries with abundant water would have to supply water to countries suffering from water stress, despite the fact that the UN has never obligated one country to provide resources to another (although it does set up programs for countries to help each other in attaining goals).

There has been some headway, however, since that historic resolution was passed. The United Nations has worked to ensure that the resolution has action. This can be seen in the UN's 2030 agenda for sustainable development, which includes seventeen Sustainable Development Goals. These goals focus on improving the health and wellness of people around the globe in addition to reducing inequality and spurring economic growth. Sustainable Development Goal 6—Clean Water and Sanitation—attempts to set up actions to coordinate global water initiatives with the UN. Anyone can support these actions. The UN's ActNow campaign for individual action on climate change and sustainability invites all citizens to add their voices. These efforts will help accelerate action plans to provide clean water and sanitation for everyone.

By 2020, organizations like the Global Sunrise Project, which engages teens, the American University of Beirut, and others were stepping up to add their work to the UN's movement. You can learn more about those efforts, and also add your own projects and intent, at the UN-Water website. ◐

Water Stress Leads to Women in Charge

There is evidence that water projects are more effective if women participate. Women often farm alongside men in developing countries, and they are often responsible for fetching water. They are the primary decision-makers when it comes to water use in their household. That's why it is increasingly important to get women into decision-making roles for water strategies in water-stressed countries. Maria Mutagamba, Ugandan minister of state for water and the environment until 2012, was an example of the success of promoting a woman into a critical position. Prior to her death in 2017, Maria—nicknamed Mama Water Africa—developed strategies for the water sector in her country. She was the coordinator of the Global Women Leaders' Initiative for WASH (Water, Sanitation, and Hygiene). Under her guidance, Ugandans' access to safe water increased from 51 percent to 61 percent in two years.

CHAPTER 10: FROM DESALINATION TO RECLAMATION—POTENTIAL SOLUTIONS AND ACTION

FROM CONTAMINATION AND SUPPLY SHORTAGES to rising seas and unrest in water-stressed countries, our water problems are numerous, but there are still causes for hope. As is clear from the actions of the United Nations, progress can happen, but it often takes time. To figure out the way forward, let's examine some possible solutions to the water crisis and see how effective they are. We'll start with one of the most obvious—bottled water.

BOTTLED WATER IS NOT THE ANSWER

In every water crisis, from Flint, Michigan, to Hampstead, New Hampshire, bottled water has proved to be an essential source of fresh water. But bottled water isn't being used by water-stressed communities only. It's also being sold to people all over the world as an alternative to sodas and sugary drinks. It is a safe and portable way to stay hydrated anytime, anywhere.

Bottled water is big business. In fact, *Consumer Reports* says that Americans spent $31 billion on bottled water in 2018 alone.

And these days, there are a lot of options for consumers—visit any supermarket, and you'll find water from natural springs, purified water, water with vitamins, water with flavorings, and many more choices.

Bottling and selling water isn't new. Water has been bottled since the seventeenth century, when people began to believe that water from natural sources was beneficial for health. Bottled water was first sold in the United States in 1767 at a spa in Boston. But the world-wide market for bottled water really took off in the 1970s when the development of new lightweight plastics made bottled water cheap and easy to transport. Perrier branded itself "Earth's First Soft Drink" in a series of American ads between 1981 and 1987. Then, in the early 2000s, the bottled water industry turned into a real force as it became a popular global alternative to tap water, and distribution became widely available.

But as the industry grew, so did the problems that come with manufacturing bottled water. Everything—from the energy it takes to create the bottles, to recycling them, to tapping the source of the water—became controversial.

The international firm Nestlé bought the French company Perrier in 1992. It continued to purchase bottled water companies and now includes brands such as San Pellegrino, Acqua Panna, Poland Spring, and Vittel. In the United States, Nestlé has removed over 4 billion gallons (15 billion liters) of water from sites in two Michigan counties since 2000. The Michigan Citizens for Water Conservation (MCWC), a nonprofit volunteer group based in Mecosta, has fought Nestlé, arguing that the aquifers that were tapped belong to the public, and a corporation has no right to deplete them to bottle and sell water. The group says that Nestlé could end up draining the local groundwater, causing the community to have problems like the ones in Hampstead, New Hampshire.

At times, the Michigan government and courts have favored the position of the MCWC. At other times, they've made decisions in favor of Nestlé. As elections come and go and the politics of the people in office change, so have the verdicts on water rights in this multidecade battle.

Of course, Nestlé is just one of many companies buying and selling water, all of which comes from aquifers, springs, and glaciers. Similar to mineral rights, water rights can be bought and sold. But this brings us back to the milkshake problem: Too many straws in the milkshake lead to a shortage for everyone.

And there are other costs linked to bottled water. To produce the plastic bottle, it takes about three times the amount of water that the bottle ends up holding. It also takes energy, which comes with its own environmental cost. It takes millions of barrels of oil just to make the bottles for US consumption. In addition, for every ton of plastic used to create bottles, three tons of carbon dioxide are generated, which contributes adversely to climate change.

Then there's the recycling component. Unfortunately, about sixty million of these bottles end up in landfills every day in the United States. Only 30 percent of the bottles are recycled in the United States. By way of comparison, 97 percent of plastic water bottles are recycled in Norway.

These are all things to think about when choosing to purchase a bottle of water. Is bottled water the solution to our water crisis? Definitely not. While it can help with short-term emergencies, the option isn't sustainable in the long term, given the associated costs, both monetary and environmental.

There's another solution being explored, however, one that might hold some answers for dry countries like Australia: desalination. 💧

Where Does the Water for Bottled Water Come From?

The popular brands of bottled water and their sources include:

- Aquafina (owned by PepsiCo) and Dasani (owned by Coca-Cola)—These brands of treated tap water come from several cities in the United States.

- Poland Spring and Zephyrhills—Both of these Nestlé brands obtain water from springs, eight in Maine and five in Florida. The Poland Spring water is not gathered from the mouth of these springs but rather from the groundwater feeding them.

- Fiji Water—This water is bottled and filtered on the island of Fiji in the South Pacific. It is artesian water, meaning it is sourced only from a well. It is then shipped thousands of miles across the ocean.

Bans on Single-Use Water Bottles

The Australian town of Bundanoon, in New South Wales, became the first in the world to outlaw bottled water in 2009. Concord, Massachusetts, made history in 2012 when it became the first town in the United States to pass legislation banning single-serving plastic bottles, in part through the efforts of eighty-four-year-old activist Jean Hill. Other municipalities have followed in the United States and around the world. San Francisco banned plastic water bottles in 2014 and began installing outdoor water bottle refilling stations for public use. In February 2020, New York City mayor Bill de Blasio signed an executive order banning single-use plastic bottles in the city. Does your town or city have a ban on single-serving plastic bottles? If not, maybe you could lend your voice to help get one enacted.

The Dangers of Water Privatization

Pope Francis, the leader of the Roman Catholic Church, focused on the inequity of available fresh water between wealthier, industrialized nations and the global poor in his May 2015 published address, *Laudato Si': On Care for Our Common Home*. In this work, which was addressed to "every person living on this planet," not just Catholics, he wrote about clean water as a "basic and universal human right." In his 2018 World Day of Prayer for the Care of Creation address, he spoke about the dangers of water privatization, meaning treating water as a commodity. "We urgently need shared projects and concrete gestures that recognize that every privatization of the natural good of water, at the expense of the human right to have access to this good, is unacceptable."

"I came to appreciate the importance of environmental concern only after escaping from Tibet in 1959, where we always considered the environment to be pure. Whenever we saw a stream of water, for instance, there was no worry about whether it was safe to drink. Sadly, the mere availability of clean drinking water is a major problem throughout the world today."
—The Dalai Lama, speaking on the fiftieth anniversary of Earth Day in 2020

DESALINATION: A POTENTIAL SOLUTION?

Australia is one of many countries, including the United States, that have turned to desalination to create drinking water.

Desalination, also known as desal, is the process by which salts and other minerals are removed from salt water. Desalination is an ancient process, and there are three main methods used throughout the world. The oldest method is thermal distillation, a process by which water is boiled and the freshwater steam is collected. The second method utilizes an electric current that drives ions across a membrane, separating out the salt ions. The third method uses reverse osmosis—pressure moves water through a membrane, leaving the salt behind. All three methods require a lot of energy, which can be a financial drain and also harm the environment.

How Desalinization Works

Salt water has two basic elements: water and salt. Desalination separates them to provide fresh water for drinking. You can see the basics of how this works by making a simple solar still. Gather a bowl filled with salt water, an empty glass that is shorter than the height of the bowl, plastic wrap, and a weight such as a small rock. Place the empty glass in the bowl of salt water so that it remains liquid-free. Cover the bowl with plastic wrap and position the rock over the glass, then place the bowl in a sunny spot. As the salt water evaporates it will leave salt crystals behind. The condensation that rises during evaporation will condense as fresh water on the plastic wrap and then fall into the empty glass. Voilà, you have made your own miniature desalination plant.

Australia began building desalination plants during a long water crisis between 2001 and 2009, caused by what has become known as the Millennium Drought. Six desal plants in the country purify water from the ocean. In 2019, as bushfires burned and contaminated Australia's water resources with toxic ash, the country used these desal plants—along with water treatment and other methods—to protect their water security. The fresh water produced by desalination, however, is a drop in the bucket for such a dry country.

Across the Indian Ocean, the dry Middle East region also employs desalination to combat water stress. Just 10 miles (16 kilometers) from Tel Aviv, Israel, Mediterranean seawater flows through a huge pipe into large concrete reservoirs. It is filtered through several feet of sand before going through the process of reverse osmosis to remove its salt. The seawater is transformed by desalination into drinking water for over 1.5 million people.

The Sea of Galilee, long a significant source of natural water for Israel, dropped to dangerously low levels in 2001. The country got to work to refill the sea, rivers, and springs. They used desalinated seawater, piped in from the plants, that could be used for drinking and farming. In 2016, Israel was getting 55 percent of its domestic water from desalination. By 2019, that figure had increased to 80 percent, and in 2020, desalinated water, along with higher than average rainfall, helped the Sea of Galilee reach full capacity once again.

Israel isn't the only country in the Middle East using desal to generate valuable water. Saudi Arabia produces the most desalinated fresh water in the world, using its available fossil fuels to power desal plants.

There are desal plants in the United States, too—in 2020 there were eleven in California, with ten more proposed. The Claude "Bud" Lewis Carlsbad Desalination Plant, about 35 miles (56 kilometers) north of San Diego, is the largest in California—and the United States. It is much needed in a place where it rains roughly twelve inches per year. The plant, which opened in 2015, turns 100 million gallons (378 million liters) of seawater into 50 million gallons (189 million liters) of fresh water each day. While most of the fresh water for the region comes from the snowmelt that flows into the Colorado River, the desalination plant supplies about 10 percent of the water needed for the area's 2019 population of 3.1 million people.

In total, there are about twenty thousand desal facilities around the world. In 2019, more than three hundred million people got their drinking water from desal plants. Could desal be the answer to the world's water crisis?

While desal does produce large quantities of fresh water, it comes at a high cost. The process of desalination releases large amounts of greenhouse gases, which contribute to climate change, which, in turn, contributes to droughts around the planet. It is a dangerous cycle for a world already threatened by dire water issues. Desal is also expensive. Add in the grave concerns about the danger to marine life from desal plants' intake area and from the extrasalty wastewater discharged back into the sea at the end of the process, and the cost climbs even more.

Solutions to the water crisis often come with costs that outweigh the benefits. But there are some worthy efforts that are not as costly on budgets or the environment. Some of these solutions are at work in the desert community of Tucson, Arizona.

CASE STUDY: TUCSON, ARIZONA— RECLAMATION AND RECHARGING

You know you're an Arizona native,
when . . . a rainy day puts you in a good mood.
—Marshall Trimble, quoted in *You Know You're an Arizona Native, When . . .* by Don Dedera

Among the first things one sees after touching down at Arizona's Tucson International Airport are the tall legendary saguaros. Rising above the desert sand at heights of up to sixty feet, they look as if they are reaching for the sky. These iconic cacti, which grow along just about every road in this area, are more like trees than cacti. Aside from being so tall, most have branches, like trees, and they can live as long as two hundred years in the wild.

The saguaro (*Carnegiea gigantea*) is well adapted to the dry Sonoran Desert that stretches from Arizona into Mexico. One of the most amazing things about saguaros is the way they absorb and store water in such a dry environment. Tucson gets only about twelve inches of rainfall each year—less than half the average annual rainfall in the United States—so each drop is precious.

Arizona's iconic saguaros (pronounced "sah-GWAH-rohs") symbolize the multiple ways water is acquired and used in the desert community of Tucson.

The saguaro has an intricate root system with a single, straight root, called a taproot, that grows deep into the earth to access groundwater. It also, however, has a maze of shallow roots that spread out about 3 to 5 inches (8 to 13 cm) below the soil to collect water from the surface when it falls as rain.

Saguaros absorb as much rainwater as they can hold. Pleats on their spiked green columnar surface expand like an accordion to make room for the influx of water, allowing the saguaro to store and use the water later, during dry times. At its most hydrated, a saguaro can weigh 3,200 to 4,800 pounds (1,451 to 2,177 kilograms)—about the weight of an average car—and about 85 percent of that weight is water.

Like the saguaro cactus, the people of the mountain-rimmed Sonoran Desert community have also adapted to the desert by using several ways to gather and store water. Management of such a crucial natural resource has become even more critical in recent years—in just a few generations, Arizona's water supply has drastically dwindled, thanks to massive development, a growing population of just under one million people, and climate change–induced drought.

TUCSON'S WATER HISTORY

Things were different in Tucson's early days. Back in the 1800s, most of the water in the city came from rivers and shallow wells that had to be dug only 25 feet (8 meters) deep. Then the population grew, and technology made it possible to extract water at a faster rate. But the water table dropped as more water was drawn out, making it more difficult to obtain water. Wells needed to be dug deeper and deeper over the years to reach the available groundwater below. By 1945, wells needed to be dug 75 feet (23 meters) deep to reach groundwater, and by 2019, the water table had more than tripled in distance. Wells had to be drilled 275 feet (84 meters) or more below the ground's surface to obtain water.

As with the groundwater underneath Hoosick, New York, and Hampstead, New Hampshire, the underground water source for Tucson is like a big lake that is being depleted by all the wells drawing water out. Unless more water enters the aquifer to replenish or recharge it, the water source eventually dries up.

Like the saguaro, which uses more than just its single taproot to obtain water, locals have to be creative in developing water sources in Tucson. Managing Tucson's water resources didn't happen overnight. Water conservation efforts began in the mid-twentieth century after groundwater depletion was apparent and the levels of surface water in lakes and ponds became irregular. Efforts started with private landscaping. Residents replaced green lawns requiring constant watering with native, drought-tolerant desert plants. This desert landscaping is called xeriscaping.

Around the same time, officials developed a strategy to recharge the aquifer serving the city.

RECHARGING THE AQUIFER

Without the benefit from vast quantities of rain and snow that renew the groundwater supply in places like Hoosick and Hampstead, the desert city of Tucson needed an outside water source to add water to their groundwater supply. The Central Arizona Project was designed to bring in Colorado River water by canals and pipes to recharge Tucson's groundwater supply.

Construction began in 1973 and lasted twenty years. The resulting 336-mile canal runs through the desert and farmlands and Indigenous peoples' reservations, from Lake Havasu in the north and east to Phoenix; it then continues southeast to the San Xavier reservation southwest of Tucson. It brings 1.3 billion gallons (4.9 billion liters) of water to the city every day. Each drop of water takes about nine days to get to Tucson. It takes another two weeks to filter into the aquifer, where it's stored until a Tucson resident turns on a faucet and it flows out.

The Avra Valley Basins

As a Tucson Water hydrologist, Margaret Snyder spends a lot of time at the Southern Avra Valley Storage and Recovery Project basins. At this facility, there are nine recharge basins totaling 226 acres (91 hectares). There are forty-three across Arizona in the Central Arizona Project (CAP) Recharge Program. Basin number 201, one of the largest, covers

40 acres (16 hectares) and looks like a big lake. How do the basins work? Picture a hole that you've dug on a sandy beach that is deep enough to reach water at the bottom. Now imagine adding more water to it. That's what hydrologists have done with the basins. Before the basins were dug, the water level was about 400 to 450 feet (122 to 137 meters) below the land surface. Snyder explained the recharging process of adding water to the aquifer: "We've been recharging on top of that, and that builds up a mound [of water]. It's about two hundred feet below the land surface here. So we've built up that aquifer about two hundred feet."

The Avra Basins that recharge the aquifers beneath them resemble large lakes.

WATER RECYCLING

Recharging the aquifers with Colorado River water was one way of increasing Tucson's water portfolio. More options were needed. As for the saguaro cactus, it's essential to have multiple ways of obtaining water. This is especially true for Tucson, given that the Colorado River is a limited resource; to complicate matters, it is used not only by Arizona but also six other western states and Mexico for irrigation, hydroelectric power, and drinking water. It's unclear whether the river will always be able to support the growth of these states. For Tucson, more water sources means more security, particularly as climate change makes the region drier. So, in addition to recharging the aquifers, Tucson decided to pursue water reclamation.

Water reclamation or remediation is the process of recycling water. First used in California in 1932, it can be an important asset in a community's water portfolio. In Tucson, gray water—the wastewater from sinks, showers, washing machines, and dishwashers—is cleaned at Agua Nueva (Spanish for "new water"), Tucson's waste treatment plant, using filters, microorganisms, and chemicals. Aboveground, purple-painted pipes distribute this water around Tucson.

The supercleaned water flowing through Tucson's purple pipes is not for drinking, washing, or swimming pools. Instead, it irrigates fifty public parks, sixty-five schools, the University of Arizona, over seven hundred single-family homes, and eighteen golf courses throughout the city. This saves water from being withdrawn for these purposes from the aquifer, meaning the aquifer water can be used primarily for drinking.

Irvine Purple

The special purple pipes in Arizona and other states, like Florida and California, are used to carry only recycled water. They are painted what's called Irvine purple, a hue named after the Irvine Ranch Water District in California that originated these uniquely colored pipes.

HARVESTING RAINWATER, STORMWATER, AND SNOWMELT

Recharging its aquifer and water recycling aren't the only tactics Tucson has used to address the city's water crisis. Tucson

Water, along with Tucson residents, also harvest rainwater, which can be collected from roofs, and stormwater, which drains from land after a rainfall.

The mountains that surround Tucson are covered with a thick blanket of snow each winter that melts slowly the following spring. The meltwater seeps into the ground, ending up in Tucson's groundwater. The mountains also send water gushing into already wet city streets after a storm.

"It's no longer the attitude of getting the water off the streets as fast as you can. It's now thinking of directing the water so that there is a longer-term benefit," said Timothy Thomure, director of Tucson Water. A hydrologist, he understands the intricacies of reclamation and the recovery of water in his Sonoran Desert community.

Tucson relies on two different kinds of water harvesting—passive, which pretty much works on its own without people involved, and active, which requires human effort.

Passive harvesting can take the form of just adding mulch to the soil. This absorbent material—which may include leaves, bark, and other natural plant matter—will soak up rainwater and hold it like a sponge to retain the soil's moisture. Changing the land by reshaping it with rocks, berms, or plantings can also form areas to channel water. For example, stones used to create small barricades around trees can keep water from flowing away from thirsty roots.

As for active harvesting, rainwater that falls on roofs and yards can be captured in rain gutters that flow into large containers called cisterns. The collected water can be used for washing, flushing toilets, watering gardens, and needs other than quenching thirst. When Tucson residents use cisterns, their water bills decrease because less city water is involved.

The water company also offers rebates and programs that enable city residents to set up cisterns on their property.

Residents have also learned to slow down the flow of water in nearby washes, or streambeds, after storms. Watershed Management Group, a nonprofit collection of activists and organizations based in Tucson, moves large boulders into washes to create channels and dams that give the fast-flowing water a chance to slow down so the ground can absorb it. In addition to recharging the groundwater and restoring Tucson's heritage of flowing creeks and rivers, this effort decreases the erosion that occurs with fast-moving runoff. This ancient restoration technique, which originated with the people of the Zuni Pueblo in New Mexico, was made accessible by the so-called stream whisperer Bill Zeedyk as a way to deal with erosion. Zeedyk, retired from the US Forest Service, wrote about his induced meandering concept in many articles and his book *Let the Water do the Work: Induced Meandering, an Evolving Method for Restoring Incised Channels,* published in 2014.

THE CHALLENGE CONTINUES

Tucson has adopted several creative strategies for conserving water, but the city still faces challenges. If the climate continues to warm, new measures will need to be added to the current ones to keep Tucson a livable community. ◗

"The word *drought* may be even losing meaning. Drought is a departure from a normal, wetter state. If the state we have now is normal and only getting worse, then drought is worse than that."
—Timothy Thomure, director of Tucson Water

Urban Heat Island

The mountains surrounding Tucson form what are known as sky islands, where cooler temperatures and higher altitudes create a distinct ecosystem. But there are also heat islands that have their own unique ecosystem. Urban heat islands occur when cities are much warmer than the surrounding nonurban areas. They are caused by excess pavement and concrete that absorbs, rather than reflects, heat. Ways to combat the increase in temperature include adding green roofs, trees, cool roofs that reflect sunlight, and pavement materials that reduce stormwater runoff and remain cooler. Urban development can also be combined with conservation to protect the natural environment. Tucson is looking at all these options to cool down the city and make it healthier for residents.

Tucson Serves as an Example

Tucson has been so successful with water management that representatives from communities around the globe have visited the city to learn firsthand how its residents are doing it. In September 2017, Lucinda Jooste, a water reuse specialist from South Africa, visited Arizona during the Annual WateReuse Symposium. She said in a subsequent article published in *MechChem Africa* that she was fascinated "to see what is possible when water reclamation forms part of planning to increase water supply to a water scarce region."

Minnesota, "Land of 10,000 Lakes," also found Tucson to be a good model. Even though it is water rich, the state's water management strategies might be unsustainable. Good water management techniques can improve any region.

As our planet continues to warm, more and more people will have to find ways to adapt to life with less water. Like the Tucson saguaros, we will need to have options and a varied water portfolio to meet these challenges head-on. Tucson's innovative strategies serve as an example for all of us.

CHAPTER 11: HOW YOU CAN MAKE A DIFFERENCE

WE'VE EXPLORED ISSUES of water quality and quantity. We've explored how water stress leads to conflict and migration. We've also detailed how governments and nations are responding. But what can we do as citizens?

Even though it might not seem like one person can make a difference, you can—from efforts that include conserving water in your own home to helping others in your community or around the globe. One voice raised can inspire change, encourage others, and help keep us all healthier. Here are several ways to get involved, from conservation to activism.

CONSERVATION FIRST!

If there's a global water shortage, the first thing we can do is try to use less water and stop being wasteful. We should use only what we really need so there's more to go around. And don't wait for a crisis in your area to begin conserving—it's better to be proactive. Start now.

You might not think you use much water but consider this: Americans use roughly 322 billion gallons (1.2 trillion liters) of water a day according to a 2015 US Geological Survey. That's on average 300 gallons (1,135 liters) per day for each household.

But that's not all. Water is also used to produce the food we eat and the products we use daily. Look at what you're wearing. It can take over 700 gallons (2,650 liters) of water to grow the half pound of cotton for one T-shirt and over 2,000 gallons (7,571 liters) for the pound and a half of cotton used for a pair of jeans. Even more water is needed to make the energy to run the sewing machines and dye the fabric for manufacturing the apparel.

As groundwater is depleted and drought challenges many communities, conservation efforts can help. Your effort might just decrease the number of sinkholes in your Florida community, decrease the amount of brackish water replacing fresh groundwater in your Texas community, or help maintain your community's groundwater level. No matter where you live, every gallon of water counts.

There are many steps we can take each day to reduce our water footprint. Each step, no matter how small, makes a difference. These are a few of the easiest:

- Take shorter showers. You can save gallons of water by taking a five-minute shower instead of an eight-minute shower.

- Flush toilets less frequently.

- Make sure pipes and faucets don't leak.

- Turn the tap off when you brush your teeth.

- Run your dishwasher only when it is full.

- Harvest water in a rain barrel or cistern, like the residents of Tucson do, and use what you harvest to water your garden.

Make a Rain Barrel

Using a rain barrel or cistern is a practical, low-cost way to collect water that falls from your roof to use later. It also has the benefit of reducing the quantity and speed of stormwater runoff that could overflow creeks. Some of these systems can be installed beside your house. Others can be dug into the ground so that you don't even see them. Find out whether your community has a program to help you obtain a cistern, or follow these instructions to make your own.

What you'll need:

- a lidded plastic garbage pail or rain barrel

- watertight sealant or plumber's tape

- two rubber washers and two metal/plastic nuts

- a spigot

- a drill

- a sheet of landscaping fabric

1. Drill a hole near the bottom of your garbage pail or rain barrel and leave enough space for a watering can or bucket beneath it.

2. Add a metal/plastic nut with rubber washer to the threaded end of the spigot.

3. Spread sealant over the rubber washer, then insert the spigot into the hole from outside the garbage pail or rain barrel.

4. Inside the garbage pail or rain barrel—attach a rubber washer to the threads of the spigot inside the barrel, and then install a metal/plastic washer over the threads.

5. Tighten the two nuts to hold the spigot in place.

6. Cut a hole in the lid of the garbage pail or rain barrel slightly larger than the downspout so that water can run in.

7. Cover the opening of the garbage pail or rain barrel with a sheet of landscaping fabric to prevent bugs from entering your water. Place the lid on top of the pail or barrel to hold the landscaping fabric in place.

8. Set your garbage pail or rain barrel underneath your home's downspout so that rain will run through the landscaping fabric and into the barrel.

As we try to reduce water usage, we must also think about the many ways we use water indirectly. Here are a few ways to conserve water that we use without even realizing it:

- **Use less energy:** It takes a lot of water to make energy. It also takes a lot of water to condense the steam and cool the mechanical and electrical components in power plants. Thousands and thousands of gallons of water are taken from wells, rivers, and oceans for energy purposes. By using less electricity, we use less water. Decreasing your electricity use is easy: Turn lights off when you leave a room. Unplug chargers when you aren't using them. Use appliances in energy-saving mode. Use efficient energy-saving light bulbs.

- **Shop wisely for clothing, buy less, and recycle and reuse when possible:** Cotton is a very thirsty crop. Although it is a natural fiber and less harmful to the environment than using fibers like polyester that require fossil fuel, growing it requires lots of water. Drawing water for the irrigation of cotton and other crops is blamed for the loss of the Aral Sea, a large freshwater lake in

Central Asia. Once the fourth-largest lake in the world, it now covers only about 10 percent of its original area. Fortunately, there are several ways the fashion industry is reducing its water footprint, and you can help, too: Search out clothing, towels, and bed linens made from less thirsty crops, like monocle, linen, bamboo, and eucalyptus. Buy clothing that will last (and you'll love) for a long time. Buy recycled and upcycled items when you want something new in your wardrobe. Or have a clothing swap with your friends. You'll save money while saving water!

- **Wash clothes less often:** They'll stay in better shape, and you'll use less water. Try airing out your jeans instead of frequently washing them.

Creating a Useful Urban Water Cycle

Cities have a lot of impervious pavements that prevent water from soaking into the earth. Water is lost as it falls on those pavements, flows into drains, and heads out into rivers and oceans. But if those urban areas start to replace some of that pavement with porous materials, such as paving stones that leave spaces for water to seep into the earth, they will benefit from being cooler—and the water will be added to underlying aquifers and help nurture healthier trees. Portland, Oregon, is one US city that has implemented that strategy. If you live in an urban area, you can help make a difference by contacting your elected officials to request this kind of change in your city.

PROTECTING OUR WATER QUALITY

The choices we make each day affect not only the amount of water available to us but also the quality of that water. There are many ways that we can keep our water cleaner, safer, and free of contaminants that can harm animals, ecosystems, and humans.

Let's start with our clothing. Aside from using gallons of water, cotton crops also account for a great deal of the pesticide used worldwide. We've already detailed how agricultural chemicals—including pesticides, herbicides, and fertilizers—can wash into and pollute waterways. Shopping for organic fibers that are farmed without these chemicals helps prevent contaminants from entering our water sources.

Polyester is a human-made product created from chemicals like ethylene glycol and is basically a sort of plastic. It is a product of the petroleum industry, and its production pollutes the environment. In addition, every time you wash polyester clothing, hundreds (or possibly *thousands*) of plastic microfibers end up in the environment, including in our water.

Plastic also ends up in our water systems when we use body and face washes and other products that contain microbeads. Tiny microplastics from these products end up in our water, and even in the fish we eat. By eliminating products that use polyester and microbeads, we can improve our water quality.

INSPIRING WATER WARRIORS

In the midst of every water crisis, there are individuals who take a stand. Some write to their elected officials. Some join a protest. Some create something transformative from their hardships. Along the way, their voices and actions push for change and justice. These are some of the individuals who have seen a problem and then taken action. They stepped forward to support their communities while inventing new ways to help. These warriors may inspire you to raise your own voice, contribute ideas, and make a difference.

Mark Baldwin, Community Gardener

As food stores closed during the water crisis in Flint, Michigan, resident Mark Baldwin decided to combat the city's food shortage and create something long lasting to benefit local kids. "We have kids who are watching," he said in 2018.

He built a hoop house greenhouse structure to grow vegetables in the vacant lot next to his home and turned it into a place where kids could learn about growing food. It wasn't easy—as crime increased during the water crisis, vandals stole Mark's equipment, destroyed his tomato plants, and set fire to the hoop house. But Mark refused to quit. He harvested rainwater for his crops to avoid using poisoned municipal water and invited community groups to bring kids to learn how to garden and improve their diets by eating healthy food. Mark made a difference to the kids in his ward, one vegetable at a time.

Grow Your Own Garden

When Mark Baldwin decided to establish a community garden next to his house, he had to make sure he gardened safely during the Flint water crisis.

If you have found lead in your water, you can still follow Mark's example and create a garden. Before you start, have your soil tested. The results will tell you if you have lead in your soil. If the lead levels are 400 ppm or lower, you can safely plant tomatoes, peppers, corn, beans, squash, cucumbers, and peas without fear of ingesting the lead. If your soil measures 300 ppm or higher, do not plant leafy greens, like lettuces and spinach, or root crops, like carrots, potatoes, turnips, and beets. Those foods will soak up the lead.

Collect water for your garden in a rain barrel or use a lead filter on your garden hose rather than using the tainted water from your home. Don't eat any vegetables that you have canned during a lead crisis unless you have taken these precautions.

Tiara Darisaw, Founder of Children for Flint

Tiara Darisaw—daughter of LaShaya Darisaw, one of the Flint moms who traveled to Hoosick, New York, in a show of solidarity—was nine years old when the citywide disaster began in Flint. Before the public knew about the toxic water, young Tiara used to visit her grandmother's home in Flint after school and take baths there. She developed rashes along her arms and across her back.

As soon as she found out how dangerous lead poisoning is to a child's brain development, Tiara began to worry. Her concern wasn't just about herself. She worried about the health of any children she might have someday—and even her possible grandkids. How would this poison affect them?

Tiara also noticed that, unlike the adults who could vote and run for office to effect change, she and her friends didn't have a voice. She knew that kids needed to be able to speak up, too, and learn about the process of politics. So she focused her energy on spreading hope to her classmates and friends by founding the organization Children for Flint.

Teens like Tiara Darisaw are instrumental in raising awareness that leads to action.

Tiara spoke up wherever she could, whether to a packed room of over five hundred journalists or to her friends in school. Tiara joined with other Flint residents—moms, activists, journalists, water scientists, and members of the medical community—to inform residents and engage in local discussions. The poised young teen was still years too young to vote—but not too young to have her voice heard and make a difference.

And Tiara wasn't alone in her efforts. Other Flint kids also spoke out. They raised their voices and wrote letters. When she was eight years old, Mari Copeny, aka Little Miss Flint, wrote a letter to President Obama about the crisis her city was facing.

"Letters from kids like you are what make me so optimistic for the future. I hope to meet you next week, 'Little Miss Flint,'" President Obama replied that April. He made good on that promise when he visited Flint in May 2016.

Mari Copeny hasn't stopped fighting for clean water. In September 2019, the twelve-year-old started #WednesdaysForWater, a hashtag on Twitter, with the intention of sharing a place in need of clean water and ways to get involved with helping. She and Tiara are making a difference in their community.

Flint Community Lab

Tiara Darisaw is one of many teens who have stepped up in Flint to make a difference. In the summer of 2018, fifteen Flint teens completed 170 water tests in Flint homes. They found that 30 percent of the homes were still without working water filters, and many homes had elevated lead levels of up to 33 ppb, much higher than the 15 ppb limit. These teens are part of a program called the Flint Community Lab, which was founded by Freshwater Future and the Flint Development Center; it received a 2020 US Water Alliance Water Prize for Outstanding Cross-Sector Partnership. The lab's purpose is to provide facts for residents and inspire community members to get involved. Its vision is to provide no-cost testing to every Flint home. This community effort can serve as a model for other impacted cities around the globe. Learn more about this great organization and get ideas for your own community at the website for the McKenzie Patrice-Croom Flint Community Lab.

Gitanjali Rao and Deepika Kurup, Young Inventors

Seventh grader Gitanjali Rao was home in Lone Tree, Colorado, over 1,000 miles (1,609 kilometers) west of Flint, Michigan, when she heard about Flint's water crisis. She saw the lead situation appear in the news over and over, with no significant changes. Then she heard about other schools in the country that were also facing rising lead levels.

"That is when I thought I could try a solution that may help others," said Gitanjali.

She wondered what would happen if people could find out if their water was contaminated before problems began. She watched her parents try to test the water in their homes. Because the testing was difficult, she assumed harmful water was going untested in many homes and schools.

Gitanjali wanted to make it easier for families to test their water right out of their tap instead of having to take it to a laboratory. It took her three months to develop a device to do just that. She named her invention Tethys, after the Greek goddess of fresh water.

Here's how her device works: When Tethys is dipped in water, lead molecules bind to chloride elements in the device. The lead can then be measured. And Gitanjali even went one step further by developing an app to deliver test data directly to a user's smartphone.

In 2017, she entered her idea for Tethys in the Discovery Education 3M Young Scientist Challenge, open to fifth- through eighth-grade students, and was selected as a finalist. She was then connected to a mentor and manufacturer, both ready to provide help with her invention. Tethys was on its way.

Deepika Kurup, from New Hampshire, was also a Discovery Education 3M Young Scientist Award winner. In eighth grade, she invented a solar-powered water purification system. Two years later, she received the US Stockholm Junior Water Prize, the world's most prestigious youth award for water-related STEM (science, technology, engineering, and mathematics) projects.

Can you invent something to help provide clean water? Enter the annual 3M Young Scientist Challenge with your invention, and you just might become a winner, too. For more information, check out the Annual Challenge/Young Scientist Lab website.

Darlene Arviso, the Water Lady
The Navajo Nation covers more than 27,000 square miles (69,930 square kilometers) across the states of New Mexico, Utah, and Arizona. It is the second-largest tribal population in the United States and has more than thirty-two thousand enrolled members.

Nearly 40 percent of Navajo homes do not have running water. Many residents rely on springs, unregulated wells, or livestock troughs to meet their needs. Forty of every one hundred Navajo people in the United States have to carry water into their homes bucket by bucket for cleaning, cooking, drinking, and bathing. For so many Navajo, the nearest water source is a round trip of over 100 miles (160 kilometers). Without a car to access it, that water is unattainable. That's where Darlene Arviso, known as the Water Lady, comes in.

Darlene loads up her yellow tanker truck and takes water to people throughout the vast Navajo reservation. Even though she can get to some families only once a month, Darlene is out on the road every day. She fills the containers the families have—buckets, barrels, and jars.

Are there people near you who don't have water? What can you do to help?

Autumn Peltier, Water Protector

Autumn Peltier is an Eagle Clan Anishinabek from Wikwemikong Unceded Territory in Northern Ontario, Canada. She is also the grand-niece of Josephine Mandamin, a founding member of the water protectors movement who walked more than 10,560 miles (17,000 kilometers) around the Great Lakes to advocate for clean water in 2003.

Autumn is following in Josephine's footsteps as an outspoken water protector. She began advocating for water conservation in 2012 when she was eight years old, and she gained a following when, in 2016, she confronted Canadian Prime Minister Justin Trudeau on his record of water protection. In 2017, at age thirteen, she was nominated for the first of three consecutive years for the International Children's Peace Prize. She has also spoken at the Assembly of First Nations and the United Nations. Autumn is a powerful inspiration to others young and old.

JOIN A WATER-PROTECTING ORGANIZATION

You don't have to go it alone. There are many organizations that are set up to help people around the world overcome water issues. Some help with improving quality and others with protecting quantity. Here are a few to check out.

Charity: water Birthday Parties

There are so many kids throughout the world who lack clean water and sanitation. The charity: water organization enables you to help them by planning a birthday fundraiser for your special day. The organization will use 100 percent of the money donated to fund clean water projects around the world. When completed, you will be notified of the projects that used your money, and charity: water will send you photos (and even the GPS locations) of those you helped. The organization claims that the average capital raised is $770, which provides thirty-eight people with clean water through the installation of water systems and the funding of water projects. To find out more and get involved, visit the charity: water website.

DigDeep/Navajo Water Project

Indigenous people in Arizona and New Mexico were not allowed to vote until 1948. They lacked a voice when water projects were allocated. Now, DigDeep is helping bring water to the Navajo and to other tribes—as well as people around the globe. The project develops new sources where water is pumped, treated, and stored. It also provides home water systems that supply families with hot and cold running water. Each week, twelve families in New Mexico can turn on their tap for the first time thanks to DigDeep's Navajo Water Project. Donations can provide water delivery for families. Whether you want to plan a fundraiser or learn how else to help, the Navajo Water Project website provides useful tips.

Seth Maxwell's Thirst Project

When US actor and movie producer Seth Maxwell learned in 2008 that over a million people worldwide didn't have clean water, he and some of his friends formed Thirst Project, one of the world's leading water activism organizations for youth. The organization funded the creation and installation of biosand filters for families in India to help them improve their water quality and is also financing well projects in Uganda and El Salvador. To help fund one of these projects visit the Thirst Project website.

Water.org

This nonprofit was cofounded by actor Matt Damon and engineer Gary White in 2009. It provides access to safe water and sanitation for communities in Africa, Asia, Latin America, and the Caribbean. By building wells and providing hygiene training to communities, the organization helps people survive and thrive. Water.org helped its first million people by 2012 and is still going strong.

You can join the global effort by holding a fundraiser. A donation of just $12.50 provides funding for projects that give people around the globe lasting access to safe water or sanitation: For more information, check out Water.org.

GOING FORWARD

It's difficult to hear about citywide water contaminations, supply shortages, droughts, and other water crises in the news, along with the conflicts that can result from these crises. Some days it seems easier to turn the news off altogether. But turning the bad news off doesn't make these disturbing water stories go away. And if we tune out, we risk missing good news as well.

In 2020, US climate and water scientist Peter Gleick tweeted that the per-person use of water in the United States—for everything from urban use to energy and even agriculture—had dropped to levels of the 1930s. Talk about promising news! It seems that we are moving in the right direction. And during the COVID-19 pandemic in 2020, with fewer tourists in Venice, cleaner water flowed through the city's canals—so clean that marine life increased. This is just one example that demonstrates we can decrease pollution, and it shows us how the earth can regenerate when it isn't overtaxed.

Of course, there are still plenty of challenges ahead. Water crises, after all, remain in the news daily. We know that as the planet's human population grows, our demand for fresh water also increases. Climate change only complicates the situation further. But we have seen how resilient we can be when challenged. We can all make a difference if we are well informed and take action. Our future will be decided by the decisions we make today.

Have the stories of water warriors inspired you? Perhaps you'll email a public official, plan a birthday-party fundraiser, or host a clothes swap. Maybe you'll imagine the next great invention that will protect us from water contamination. Or maybe one day you will run for office and make important water legislation happen. Each action you take to combat the water crisis, no matter how small or insignificant it may seem, makes a difference.

This is our world. We must protect it for our survival and for future generations. We are all in this together. 💧

ACKNOWLEDGMENTS

As we've seen, water stress significantly affects many communities worldwide. I spent a great deal of time speaking with people facing these difficult and dangerous situations while researching this book. Those encounters were eye-opening, frightening, and heartbreaking. My gratitude to SEJ for making so many of these possible.

I sat with my mom the day after I came home from Flint. I shared my experiences there, as difficult and enlightening as they were. She was my inspiration for this book. She fought hard to keep our drinking water free from additives when I was a child growing up in New York's Rockland County. I remember walking door-to-door with her to get petitions signed. Thanks to her and others, Rockland's water remains fluoride-free. She taught me to use my voice, stand up for what I believe—and know that each of us can make a difference. This book is dedicated to her memory.

I want to thank all the people who have shared their stories with me—the people of Flint, Hoosick, Hampstead, Tucson, Venice, Louisiana, the Navajo Nation, and others. So many of them have suffered in innumerable ways but have also used their experiences to support other communities. They shined a light on a very dark subject and changed my worldview. I am eternally grateful.

Four months after my visit to Flint, I received terrible news. Jassmine had become one of the youngest victims of the city's water crisis. After suffering for four years, the thirty-year-old passed away in February 2019. She became yet another casualty in the world's water crisis. I was, and still am, heartbroken. This book is dedicated to her memory also.

Along this book's steep path, there were also moments of joy, like hearing of small victories from Deanna Anthony. I am grateful to her for sharing her story with me.

While in Tucson, I spent the day walking in the washes and seeing the results of a spring storm with my former neighbor, Stuart Chaney. I thank him for introducing me to Zuni bowls and the beautiful native Arizona ecosystems.

I also want to thank Valerie Herman and my tour guides from Tucson Water; my daughter, Lucie, who shared stories and photos of her trip to India's Ganga Mata; Judith Enck, for answering my endless questions; Circle of Blue; and all the people I met who are fighting for clean water.

The team behind the publishing of this book remained supportive through some tough times. I'm grateful to Algonquin Young Readers, including Elise Howard and Krestyna Lypen, who persevered through the pandemic to bring this important book to my readers.

It takes a village to create a book, and my village is filled with the best people. I'm always thankful to my writer buds who lend an ear through my book journeys, including Anita Sanchez, Lois Huey, Judy Bryan, Leslie Helakoski, Carrie Pearson, and many other SCBWI friends. I am grateful to my valiant agent, Jennifer Laughran, for her ever-present support.

Lastly, my endless gratitude to my husband, Dean, who is always by my side for it all . . . to the last drop.

GLOSSARY

acid mine drainage—runoff water that becomes contaminated by heavy metals during mining activities

aquifer—an underground source of water that lies between layers of rock, gravel, or sand

chelation therapy—a medical procedure for removing metals such as lead from the bloodstream

desertification—the process by which fertile land becomes too degraded to support crops

drought—a long period of little or no rainfall that leads to dry land and a shortage of water

extraction—the process of removing natural resources such as oil, gas, coal, water, or minerals from the earth

fracking—the process by which natural gas or oil is extracted from the earth by way of high-powered liquid drilling

gray water—water that drains from sinks, showers, dishwashers, and washing machines

groundwater—water that lies beneath the surface of the earth

irrigation—the process of watering crops

nonpoint source pollution—a type of pollution that does not pass directly into a water source, such as runoff from cropland, streets, and lawns

oxidation—a chemical reaction that occurs during mineral mining and eventually leads to acid mine drainage, which can poison water

PFAS—for *per- and polyfluoroalkyl substances,* industrial chemicals (including PFOA) that pollute waterways and can cause cancer in humans

PFOA—for *perfluorooctanoic acid*, an industrial chemical that pollutes waterways

point source pollution—an identifiable source of pollution, such as a ship drain or factory smokestack

pollution—a harmful substance that can cause damage to the environment

recharge—to add water to an aquifer to renew the supply

sewage—wastewater flushed into a public drainage system

turbidity—a measure of a liquid's clarity

wash—a dry desert streambed

wastewater—water from sewers, industry, and agricultural runoff

xeriscape—a landscape that uses water-saving techniques instead of irrigation

RESOURCES

All water has a perfect memory and is forever trying to get back to where it was.
—Toni Morrison, Nobel laureate and American author

ANNUAL DATES TO OBSERVE

March 22, World Water Day: Check out resources and activities on the World Water Day website, www.worldwaterday.org, and follow #WorldWaterDay on social media.

October 23, Imagine a Day Without Water: To participate, sign up on the Imagine a Day Without Water website, imagineadaywithoutwater.org, and follow #DayWithoutWater on social media.

November 19, World Toilet Day: For more information and programs, visit the World Toilet Day website, www.worldtoiletday.info, and follow #WorldToiletDay on social media.

Follow these hashtags for more water news:
#water
#WaterIsLife
#drought
#cleanwater

WATCH

An Inconvenient Truth (2006). Paramount.
Former Vice President Al Gore's informative documentary explores climate change.

An Inconvenient Sequel: Truth to Power (2017). Actual Films.
Al Gore returns after his original documentary with an update to show viewers where we are now in the throes of climate change and what needs to be done.

Before the Flood (2016). Killer Content, National Geographic Channel.
Leonardo DiCaprio produced this riveting account of climate change events around the globe.

Dark Waters (2019). Todd Haynes, Nathaniel Rich, Mario Correa, Mark Ruffalo, Anne Hathaway, Tim Robbins. Focus Features. The story dramatizes Robert Bilott's case against the chemical manufacturing corporation DuPont for a town contaminated by PFOA.

Erin Brockovich (2000). Steven Soderbergh, Susannah Grant, Julia Roberts. Universal Pictures. This movie tells the true story of legal assistant Erin Brockovich's work to bring down a California power company accused of contaminating a town's water supply.

"Fracking 101." Narrated by Edward James Olmos. Sierra Club. This fracking video shows the basics of the process. https://www.youtube.com/watch?v=5TTQI03D9Vc&feature=emb_logo

Lowland Kids: Growing Up on a Disappearing Island (2019). RYOT Films x HuffPost Short Stories Doc. Directed by Sandra Winther. The story of the last teenagers living on a vanishing island on the coast of Louisiana. https://www.youtube.com/watch?v=tHV0F3-72Eo

READ

Castaldo, Nancy F. *River Wild: An Activity Guide to North American Rivers*. Chicago Review Press, 2008. Rivers provide water throughout the world. This book focuses on the rivers of North America. It also features people who help keep them clean.

Estes, Nick and Jhaskiran Dhillon editors. *Standing with Standing Rock: Voices from the #NODAPL Movement*. University of Minnesota Press, 2019. This book provides insight into how Standing Rock youth led the call, and millions around the world answered it.

Gore, Al. *An Inconvenient Truth: The Crisis of Global Warming*. Rodale Press, 2006. This book supplements the documentary.

LaDuke, Winona. *To Be a Water Protector: The Rise of the Windigoo Slayers*. Fernwood Publishing, 2020. This book explores activism at Standing Rock, the new green economy, and other issues.

Park, Linda Sue. *A Long Walk to Water: Based on a True Story*. Clarion Books, 2011. This story focuses on how two young people—one in 1985 and the other in 2008—face water challenges in Sudan.

Shusterman, Neal, and Jarrod Shusterman. *Dry*. Simon & Schuster Books for Young Readers, 2018. Could you imagine a world without water? This young adult dystopian novel reveals what the future might hold if we don't change course.

ACTIVITIES

Look at the Environmental Working Group's PFAS (per- and polyfluoroalkyl substances) contamination map of the United States to find out where toxic areas are most likely to be found: https://www.ewg.org/interactive-maps/pfas_contamination/map/

Solve Central Arizona Project's Water Math Puzzle at www.cap-az.com/documents/education/games/activity-5.html

Examine water quality reports from Newark, New Jersey, and Hoosick Falls, New York, at https://waterandsewer.newarknj.gov/annual-water-quality-reports and https://www.villageofhoosickfalls.com/Water/testing.html, then look at the reports from your area.

SOURCE NOTES

"The twentieth century was about oil": Erin Brockovich. Twitter, @ErinBrockovich, June 24, 2019. https://twitter.com/ErinBrockovich/status/1143204481456361473?s=20
"Spring water is justice": Karin Boye, "Spring Water," 2017.

INTRODUCTION

"We give thanks to all the waters": National Museum of the American Indian, "Haudenosaunee Thanksgiving Address," November 2018, 2015 https://blog.nmai.si.edu/main/2015/11/haudenosaunee-thanksgiving-address.html.
"little to no authentic future": Visalia, CA: Tulare County Planning Department, 1973. "County of Tulare General Plan: Water and Liquid Waste Management, Policies, Programs," p. 2.

CHAPTER ONE

"The effects of lead is insidious": Bryant, Bunyan. "The Menace of Lead." http://www-personal.umich.edu/~bbryant/poems1.html.
"So later this spring, we will all be drinking Pure Flint Michigan Natural Mineral Water": Walling, Dayno, State of the City Speech, March 3, 2014. http://media.mlive.com/newsnow_impact/other/Mayor%20Walling's%20State%20of%20the%20City%20Address%20030314.pdf
"We expect that the Flint Water Treatment Plant will be fully operational": Lynch, Jim, Jonathan Oosting and Chad Livengood. "2 Flint Employees, EM OK'd River Water Plan." *Detroit News*, Feb. 29, 2016. https://www.detroitnews.com/story/news/michigan/flint-water-crisis/2016/02/29/flint-employees-em-river-water-plan/81100790/
"If we put enough fires to the kettle": Ivory, Tia. Personal interview, Flint, MI, October 4, 2018.
"She's my miracle": Jacqueline McBride. Personal interview, October 4, 2018.
"You've got to put first and last month's rent down": Boseman, Julie. "Many Flint Residents Are Desperate to Leave but See No Escape." *New York Times*, Feb. 5, 2016. https://www.nytimes.com/2016/02/05/us/many-flint-residents-are-desperate-to-leave-but-see-no-escape.html
"WOW! MAYOR WEAVER'S FAST START INITIATIVE HAS EXCAVATED": Personal observation, Flint, MI, Oct. 2018.
"Because of Flint, there has been an incredible ripple effect": Hanna-Attisha, Mona. Lecture attended, Flint, MI, Oct. 3, 2018.
"necessity to build a village of folks": Hanna-Attisha, Mona. Lecture attended, Flint, MI, Oct. 3, 2018.
"Water has not contributed in any significant way": Ras Baraka to Anna Werner, *CBS This Morning*, Nov. 1, 2018. https://www.cbsnews.com/news/newark-new-jersey-water-lead-contamination/

"Once residents know the truth about Newark's water quality": Apr. 26, 2018 statement—City of Newark. https://www.facebook.com/CityofNewark/posts/statement-from-the-city-of-newark-directorof-water-and-sewer-utilities-andrea-ad/862821337257987/

"We also are troubled that Newark": Olson, Erik. "Newark Is Still Leaving Thousands Without Safe Water." NRDC Expert Blog, Oct. 18, 2019. https://www.nrdc.org/experts/erik-d-olson/newark-leaving-thousands-without-safe-water

"fights to liberate clean water as a source of life for all": Newark Water Coalition mission statement. https://www.newarkwatercoalition.com/

"NEW Caucus and other residents stood up to fight": "Major Settlement Reached in Newark Tap Water Lead Case," NRDC, January 21, 2021, https://www.nrdc.org/media/2021/210126

"Everyone has a right to safe drinking water": NRDC Press Release. "NRDC Statement at the Conclusion of the Newark Drinking Water Hearing in Federal Court." NRDC, Aug. 16, 2019. https://www.nrdc.org/media/2019/190816-0

"We're ducking and dodging bullets": Corasaniti, Nick, Corey Kilgannon and John Schwartz. "Lead Crisis in Newark Grows, as Bottled Water Distribution Is Bungled." *New York Times*, Aug. 14, 2019. https://www.nytimes.com/2019/08/14/nyregion/newark-water-lead.html

CHAPTER TWO

"I gave [government officials] hell": LaShaya Darisaw. *Capital Tonight*, Mar. 15, 2017. https://www.facebook.com/watch/?v=175633619611655

"get tired of having 500 people show up at their office": Frenette, Liza. "Mothers Share Worries and Anger over Poison Water." *NYSUT*, Oct. 7, 2016. https://www.nysut.org/news/2016/october/mothers-share-worries-and-anger-over-poison-water

"I remember having that first conversation with the mayor": Lyons, Brendan J. "A Danger that Lurks Below: In Hoosick Falls, Have Health Problems Resulted from Water Contamination?" *Times Union*, Dec. 12, 2015, updated: Mar. 15, 2016. https://www.timesunion.com/local/article/A-danger-that-lurks-below-6694498.php

"likely to be carcinogenic to humans": Environmental Protection Agency: PFAS Laws and Regulations. https://www.epa.gov/pfas/pfas-laws-and-regulations

"I told all my students to stop drinking the water": Frenette, Liza. "Mothers Share Worries and Anger over Poison Water." *NYSUT*, Oct. 7, 2016. https://www.nysut.org/news/2016/october/mothers-share-worries-and-anger-over-poison-water

"I knew I had to sell my dream house": Testimony of Emily Marpe Before the Environment and Climate Change Subcommittee of the House Committee on Energy and Commerce on "Protecting Americans at Risk of PFAS Contamination and Exposure," May 15, 2019. https://www.congress.gov/116/meeting/house/109746/witnesses/HHRG-116-IF18-Wstate-MarpeE-20190515.pdf

"It's not just a physical crisis degrading our bodies": Anna Wysocki. Transcript of Hoosick Town Meeting, July 8, 2016.

"Why won't you stop poisoning our children?": Loreena Hacket. Public Hearing, Hoosick, NY, Aug. 30, 2016.

"There is a growing water crisis in our state . . . New York": Andrew Cuomo, Dec. 20, 2018 Speech. Dewitt, Karen. "New Yorkers Affected by Drinking Water Contamination Urge

State Panel to Go Further." *WXII News*, Dec. 19, 2018. https://www.wxxinews.org/post/new-yorkers-affected-drinking-water-contamination-urge-state-panel-go-further

"It doesn't matter what your political party is": Erin Brockovich. Hoosick Falls, Jan. 30, 2016. YouTube. https://www.youtube.com/watch?v=AcGpvFTi60g

"Tastes better than what the city water does": "First These Kentuckians Couldn't Drink the Water, Now They Can't Afford It." NPR, Oct. 31, 2019. https://www.npr.org/2019/10/31/772677717/first-these-kentuckians-couldnt-drink-the-water-now-they-can-t-afford-it

"Water rates so high": "First These Kentuckians Couldn't Drink the Water, Now They Can't Afford It." NPR, Oct. 31, 2019. https://www.npr.org/2019/10/31/772677717/first-these-kentuckians-couldnt-drink-the-water-now-they-can-t-afford-it

"We know coal ash and substances like arsenic": Fernandez, Jennifer. "5 Years after Dan River Coal Ash Spill, Duke Energy Close to Finishing State-Mandated Cleanup at Site." [Greensboro, NC] *News & Record*, Feb. 1, 2019. https://www.greensboro.com/news/state/years-after-dan-river-coal-ash-spill-duke-energy-close/article_de8d0fa9-43e8-5b83-85d1-b253683a0548.html

CHAPTER THREE

"assure our Country would be independent": French, Carol. "A Dairy Farmer Shares her Story about Fracking: What Have We Done?" An Op-ed by Carol French for *PublicHerald.org*, Oct. 30, 2012. https://publicherald.org/a-dairy-farmer-shares-her-story-about-fracking-what-have-we-done/

"We have documentation from DEP that fracking and drilling": Carol French. "A Personal Story: Carol French, Bradford County, Pennsylvania." *Preserve the Beartooth Front*, June 4, 2014. https://preservethebeartoothfront.com/2014/06/04/a-personal-story-carol-french-bradford-county-pennsylvania-with-video/

"white, with a green moss settling on top": Carol French. "A Personal Story: Carol French, Bradford County, Pennsylvania." *Preserve the Beartooth Front*, June 4, 2014.

"I'm living in limbo": Carolyn Knapp. Personal phone interview, Jan. 23, 2021.

"I was born and raised in Colorado": PDC Oil and Gas TV commercial. Personally viewed in Colorado, Oct. 2018.

"This project endangers the students of Bella Romero": Nelson, Patricia. Personal interview, Greeley, CO, Oct. 2019.

"This is setting a dangerous precedent": Nelson, Patricia. Personal interview, Greeley, CO, Oct. 9, 2019.

"The harms fracking does to nearby communities": Sierra Club. "Public Health and Environmental Advocates Urge Court to Halt Fracking Next to Bella Romero Academy." June 7, 2018. https://www.sierraclub.org/press-releases/2019/04/public-health-and-environmental-advocates-urge-court-halt-fracking-next-bella

"I really think that Cullen's lockdown did shine some light": Nelson, Patricia. Personal interview, Greeley, CO, Oct. 9, 2019.

"We are governed by prayer": Cedric Goodhouse. YouTube. https://www.youtube.com/watch?v=DLHeO2aMm4U

"We are running for our lives": "Native American Youth Run to Nation's Capital from North Dakota for Rezpect Our Water Campaign." *Last Real Indians*, July 16, 2016. https://lastrealindians.com/news/2016/7/16/jul-16-2016-native-american-youth-run-to-nations-capital-from-north-dakota-for-rezpect-our-water-campaign

"We opened so many hearts and eyes and ears": https://www.youtube.com/watch?v=WwT67HnJNCk

"I watched as the United States government unleashed a level of violence": Lobe, Cullen. Personal interview, Colorado, Oct. 9, 2019.

"They understood how important water was": Redner, Trina. Personal interview, Flint, MI, Oct. 2018.

"It was really about my ancestors": Blair, Jade. "Maori Group Performs Sacred Dance at Standing Rock." *Yahoo! Finance*, Nov. 29, 2016. https://ca.finance.yahoo.com/news/maori-group-performs-sacred-dance-at-standing-rock-191632830.html

"The biggest challenge that faces Indian Country": Redner, Trina. Personal interview. Flint, MI, Oct. 2018.

"private militia spent the week of Thanksgiving shooting": Op Ed: "Thanksgiving Is a Tradition. It's Also a Lie." *Los Angeles Times*, Nov. 23, 2017. https://www.latimes.com/opinion/op-ed/la-oe-orange-thanksgiving-history-20171123-story.html

"In 1493 Spaniards used war dogs to kill Natives": Sara Sunshine Manning. Twitter @SarahSunshineM, September 3, 2016. https://twitter.com/SarahSunshineM/status/772193521641984000

"It all comes down to energy security": "Voices from Standing Rock." *Washington Post*, Dec. 12, 2016. https://www.washingtonpost.com/sf/national/2016/12/02/voices-from-standing-rock/

"We don't see eye to eye": "Voices from Standing Rock." *Washington Post*, Dec. 12, 2016. https://www.washingtonpost.com/sf/national/2016/12/02/voices-from-standing-rock/

"The Dakota Access pipeline is now officially open for business": Meyer, Robinson. Oil Is Flowing Through the Dakota Access Pipeline." *The Atlantic*, June 9, 2017. https://www.theatlantic.com/science/archive/2017/06/oil-is-flowing-through-the-dakota-access-pipeline/529707/

"This is a company under criminal investigation": Hasselman, Jan. "Standing Rock Sioux Tribe Seeks Court Ruling to Halt Pipeline Operations, as Dakota Access LLC Pushes for Expansion." https://www.standingrock.org/content/standing-rock-sioux-tribe-seeks-court-ruling-halt-pipeline-operations-dakota-access-llc

"This pipeline should have never been built here": Earthjustice. "Judge Orders Dakota Access Pipeline Shut Down." July 6, 2020. https://earthjustice.org/news/press/2020/judge-orders-dakota-access-pipeline-to-shut-down

"respect our lands and our waters, and stop this illegal pipeline." Farah, Nilna H. "Court Blocks Dakota Access. Will Biden Kill It?" *E&E News*: Oil and Gas, Jan. 27, 2021.

CHAPTER FOUR

"highly toxic to humans and wildlife": Moser, V. C. "Aldicarb." 3rd, Chapter 95, Wexler, P. (ed.), *Encyclopedia of Toxicology*. Elsevier Science, New York, NY, 1:123-125,

(2014). EPA Science Inventory. https://cfpub.epa.gov/si/si_public_record_report.cfm?Lab=NHEERL&dirEntryId=237945

"It's become obvious over the last five years that the loss of TEMIK": AgLogic Press Release. "AgLogic™ 15G Aldicarb Pesticide Available for 2016 Growing Season: Limited Quantities Available in Georgia for Initial Launch." Mar. 11, 2016. https://site.extension.uga.edu/brooksag/files/2016/03/AgLogic15G-Launch-Release-Letter.pdf

"Everything rolls downhill": Barrett, Rick. "Industrial Dairy Farming Is Taking Over in Wisconsin, Crowding Out Family Operations and Raising Environmental Concerns." *Milwaukee Journal Sentinel*, Feb. 11, 2020. https://www.jsonline.com/in-depth/news/special-reports/dairy-crisis/2019/12/06/industrial-dairy-impacts-wisconsin-environment-family-farms/4318671002/

"As a researcher of groundwater for 25 years now": Borchardt, Mark. "Study, Fecal Contamination Remains a Problem In Wells Previously Found to Be Contaminated." Associated Press, Aug. 5, 2019. https://madison.com/wsj/news/local/environment/study-fecal-contamination-remains-a-problem-in-wells-previously-found-to-be-contaminated/article_94b634a9-5ac9-53f2-bf17-8e3a173c9531.html

"This is not how we should be living": Bence, Susan. "Kewaunee County Residents Fed Up Living with Contaminated Wells." WUWM [Milwaukee], Apr. 8, 2019. https://www.wuwm.com/environment/2019-04-08/kewaunee-county-residents-fed-up-living-with-contaminated-wells

CHAPTER FIVE

"We've had some cyanobacteria outbreaks": Potvin, Lynette. Personal interview, Isle Royale, MI, June 2019.

"We've seen as many as 100 patients": Branham, William. "Florida's Toxic Red Tide Is a Perfect Storm for the Gulf Coast." *PBS News Hour*, Sept. 5, 2018. https://www.pbs.org/newshour/show/floridas-toxic-red-tide-is-a-perfect-storm-for-the-gulf-coast

CHAPTER SIX

"If you or I went to the doctor": Smith, Belinda. "Platypuses in Polluted Water Could Ingest 'Half a Human Dose' of Antidepressants." *ABC Science*, Nov. 6, 2018. https://www.abc.net.au/news/science/2018-11-07/melbourne-waterways-pharmaceuticals-pollution-spiders-platypus/10466016

"Last year, pharmaceuticals were found": Smith, Belinda. "Platypuses in Polluted Water Could Ingest 'Half a Human Dose' of Antidepressants." *ABC Science*, Nov. 6, 2018.

CHAPTER SEVEN

"It was a Monday morning": Anthony, Deanna. Personal interview, Hampstead, NH, Sept. 2018.

"We moved here in May 2018": Anthony, Deanna. Personal interview, Hampstead, NH, Sept. 2018.

"Thank goodness for the pool": Anthony, Deanna. Personal interview, Hampstead, NH, Sept. 2018.

"If it's yellow, let it mellow": Anthony, Langdon. Personal interview, Hampstead, NH, Sept. 2018.

"Groundwater represents a bank": Thomas Meixner. "Groundwater Recharge in the American West under Climate Change." *Science Daily*, Nov. 16, 2017. https://www.sciencedaily.com/releases/2017/11/171116114216.htm

"At first, the well company thought": Anthony, Deanna. Personal interview, Hampstead, NH, Sept. 2018.

"Our house is worth zero dollars": Anthony, Deanna. Personal interview, Hampstead, NH, Sept. 2018.

"You're taking our water which nobody produces": Gibson, Sarah. "In Hampstead, Residents Spar with Private Utility over Town's Water." [New Hampshire and NPR] *NHPR*, Aug. 21, 2019. https://www.nhpr.org/post/hampstead-residents-spar-private-utility-over-town-s-water#stream/0

"There is only so much a group can do": DeBerardinis, Rachel. "Hampstead Teen Pens Letter to Sununu about Town's Water Woes." [North Andover, Mass.] *Eagle-Tribune*, Dec. 12, 2018. https://www.eagletribune.com/news/new_hampshire/hampstead-teen-pens-letter-to-sununu-about-towns-water-woes/article_7e4ad713-5b23-5488-a27c-60685dd29bfd.html

"Indications are that our rainfall patterns": "South Africa Rations Water to Save Dwindling Supplies," Reuters, Oct. 28, 2019, https://www.reuters.com/article/us-safrica-drought/south-africa-rations-water-to-save-dwindling-supplies-idUSKBN1X71H0?mc_cid=8f6fb3d8ad&mc_eid=3840c9216f

"No matter how hard you work": Quackenbush, Casey. "'A Harbinger of Things to Come': Farmers in Australia Struggle with Its Hottest Drought Ever." *Time*, Feb. 21, 2019. https://time.com/longform/australia-drought-photos/

CHAPTER EIGHT

"I always talk about water as our life and our death": Comardelle, Chantel. Personal communication, Feb. 2019 (email).

"massive amounts of gardens, cattle, lots of livestock": Comardelle, Chantel. Personal communication, Feb. 2019 (email).

"We knew we had to ensure our future": Comardelle, Chantel. Personal communication, Feb. 2019 (email).

"We are not moving off the island": Vai, Cynthia. "Vanishing Isle de Jean Charles." *Portrait of June*, July, 6, 2017. https://portraitofjune.com/2017/07/06/driving-isle-de-jean-charles/

"The parquet flooring lifted right up": Caffè Florian hostess. Personal interview, Venice, Dec. 2018.

"apocalyptic devastation": "Venice on Its Knees as Floods Devastate City. " *ANSA.it*, Nov. 13, 2019. https://www.ansa.it/english/news/2019/11/13/venice-on-its-knees-as-floods-devastate-city_82b8e0ba-cdb4-4baa-83a6-4441dacc8585.html

CHAPTER NINE

"With escalating global population and the impact of a changing climate": CNA. 2017. *The Role of Water Stress in Instability and Conflict*. CRM-2017-U-016532. Final. https://www.cna.org/mab/reports

"Freshwater is so vital to the human condition": CNA. 2017. *The Role of Water Stress in Instability and Conflict.* CRM-2017-U-016532. Final. https://www.cna.org/mab/reports

"groundwater abstraction exceeds natural recharge rates": World Bank. 2017. *Beyond Scarcity: Water Security in the Middle East and North Africa.* MENA Development Series. World Bank: Washington, DC, 2018.

"If water consumption for agriculture": Radio Farda. "Iran's Water Crisis Passes Tipping Point." Dec. 13, 2017. https://en.radiofarda.com/a/iran-water-crisis-serious-soil-erosion/28914002.html

"Iran is one example of water stress": McQuaid, Julia. Personal interview, Flint, MI, Oct. 2018.

"Water is life. This water will help everyone in the region": Dowell, William. "Corps of Engineers to Raise Dahla Dam, Provide Water Essential to Southern Afghanistan." *US Army News*, Apr. 10, 2014. https://www.army.mil/article/123809/corps_of_engineers_to_raise_dahla_dam_provide_water_essential_to_southern_afghanistan

"We are reviving a region, restoring hope": "'We Are Restoring Hope': Afghan Prez, Modi Inaugurate India-Built Dam." *Hindustan Times*, June 4, 2016. https://www.hindustantimes.com/india-news/live-we-are-restoring-hope-modi-afghan-president-inaugurate-india-built-friendship-dam/story-bfJVW7Y5Oz6JgQup2SMhKN.html

"available, safe, acceptable, accessible and affordable water and sanitation." Mintz, Jesse. "The UN Votes Today on Making Clean Water a Human Right—and Canada's Voting No." This, July 28, 2010. https://this.org/2010/07/28/water-human-rights/

"Allow me to begin the presentation of this Resolution": Pablo Solón Romero, United Nations Address; full text: "UN Declares Drinking Water a Human Right." Habitat International Coalition, July 30, 2010. https://www.hic-net.org/un-declares-drinking-water-a-human-right/

CHAPTER TEN

"every person living on this planet": Pope Francis, *Laudito Si': On Care for Our Common Home.* United States Conference of Catholic Bishops, 2015. https://www.usccb.org/offices/general-secretariat/laudato-si-care-our-common-home

"We urgently need shared projects": O'Kane, Lydia. "Pope Francis: Care for Water Is Urgent Imperative." *Vatican News*, Sept. 1, 2018. https://www.vaticannews.va/en/pope/news/2018-09/pope-francis-care-for-water-is-urgent-imperative.html

"You know you're an Arizona native, when . . ." Dedera, Don. *You Know You're an Arizona Native, When . . .* (Prickly Pear Press, 1993).

"I came to appreciate the importance of environmental concern": Dalai Lama. "His Holiness the Dalai Lama's Message for Earth Day." DalaiLama.com, Earth Day, 2020. https://www.dalailama.com/news/2020/his-holiness-the-dalai-lamas-message-for-earth-day

"We've been recharging on top of that": Snyder, Margaret. Personal interview, Tucson, AZ, Feb. 2019.

"It's no longer the attitude of getting the water": Thomure, Timothy. Personal interview, Tucson, AZ, Feb. 2019.

"The word *drought* may be even losing meaning": Thomure, Timothy. Personal interview, Tucson, AZ, Feb. 2019.

"to see what is possible when water reclamation forms part of planning": "Wastewater Reclamation and the Western Cape Crisis." *MechChem Africa*, Feb. 2018. https://user-54716422671.cld.bz/MechChem-Africa-February-2018/32

CHAPTER ELEVEN

"Letters from kids like you are what make me so optimistic": Meyer, Ken. "Asked and Answered: President Obama Responds to an Eight-Year-Old Girl from Flint." Obama White House Archives, April 27, 2016. https://obamawhitehouse.archives.gov/blog/2016/04/27/asked-and-answered-president-obama-responds-eight-year-old-girl-flint

"That is when I thought I could try a solution that may help others": Rao, Gitanjali. Personal communication, March 2019 (email).

INDEX

Note: Page numbers in *italics* refer to photographs.